THE ROYAL BABY ALBUM

THE ROYAL BABY ALBUM

Diana Thomas

Arlington Books
Clifford Street Mayfair
London

THE ROYAL BABY ALBUM
First published 1984 by
Arlington Books (Publishers) Ltd
3 Clifford Street Mayfair
London W1

© Diana Thomas 1984

Typeset by Inforum Ltd Portsmouth
Colour separations by Fotographics
Printed and bound in England by
William Clowes Ltd, Beccles

British Library Cataloguing in Publication Data

Thomas, Diana
Royal baby picture album.
1. Great Britain—Kings and rulers—Children
—Biography
I. Title
929.7'2   DA28.3

ISBN 0 85140 642 4

Contents

Acknowledgements

The author and publisher would like to thank the following for their kind permission to reproduce photographs in this book.

Colour photographs

Reproduced by gracious permission of Her Majesty the Queen: 19, 26, 27, 31, 43, 62, 63, 82, 83; Camera Press: 70, 71 (Norma Short), 118 (John Scott), 119, 122, 127, 130, 131, 134, 135, 138, 139, 143; Colour Library: 47, 151, 155; Cooper Bridgeman: 106, 107; Illustrated London News: 90, 115; Newnes Group: 78, 97; Press Association: 142, 158; Time Life: 99; John Topham Picture Library: 23; Windsor Royal Library: 22, 23; Wolverhampton Art Gallery: 14, 15. *Front jacket: Top left* Crown copyright; *Centre:* Mary Evans Picture Library; *Top right:* John Topham Picture Library; *Bottom:* Camera Press. *Back jacket:* Press Association.

Black and white photographs

Crown Copyright: 66, 73, 77, 81, 87, 91, 105, 111; Camera Press: 77, 96, 13, 126; BBC Hulton Picture Library: 59, 64, 69, 80, 81, 85, 95; Mary Evans Picture Library: 11; Fox Photos: 153; Keystone: 100, 101, 140, 156; Mansell Collection: 21; Popperfoto: 17, 25, 65, 93, 95, 101, 103, 104, 108, 109, 121, 124, 125, 128, 129, 136, 145, 149; Press Association: 116, 118, 149, 152; John Topham Picture Library: 44, 96, 97, 114, 128, 133, 137, 147; Windsor Royal Archives: 29, 32, 33, 34, 35, 37, 39, 45, 48, 50, 51, 53, 54, 55, 57.

Extracts from *A King's Story* reproduced by permission Cassells & Co.

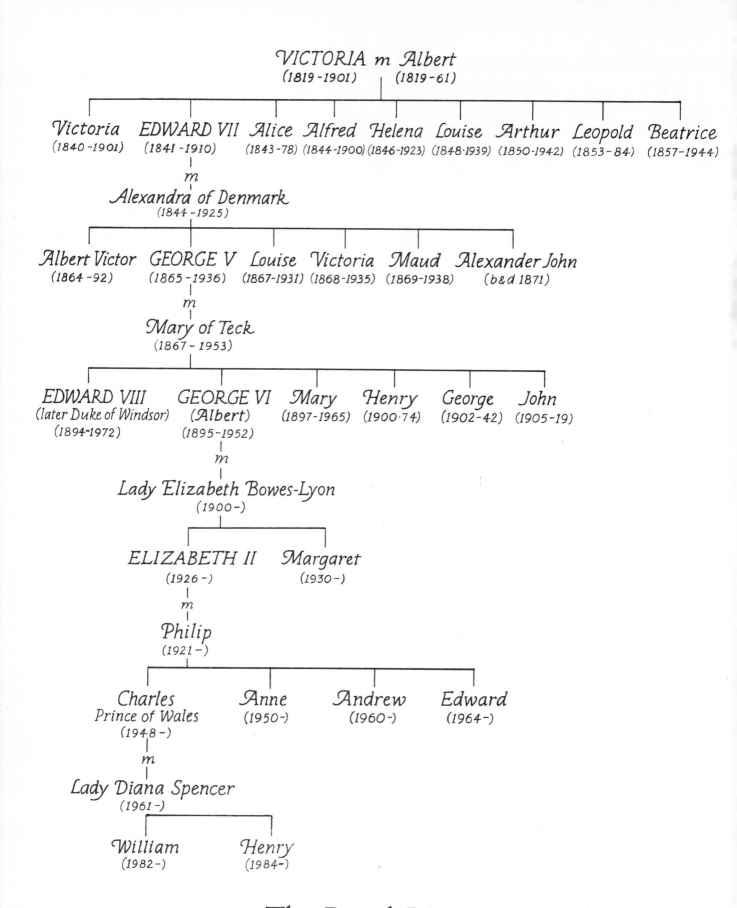

VICTORIA *m* Albert
(1819 -1901)   (1819 -61)

Victoria   EDWARD VII   Alice   Alfred   Helena   Louise   Arthur   Leopold   Beatrice
(1840 -1901)   (1841 -1910)   (1843-78)   (1844-1900) (1846-1923) (1848-1939) (1850-1942) (1853-84)   (1857-1944)

m
Alexandra of Denmark
(1844 -1925)

Albert Victor   GEORGE V   Louise   Victoria   Maud   Alexander John
(1864 -92)   (1865 -1936)   (1867-1931) (1868-1935) (1869-1938) (b & d 1871)

m
Mary of Teck
(1867 – 1953)

EDWARD VIII   GEORGE VI   Mary   Henry   George   John
(later Duke of Windsor) (Albert)   (1897-1965) (1900-74)   (1902-42)   (1905-19)
(1894-1972)   (1895-1952)

m
Lady Elizabeth Bowes-Lyon
(1900 –)

ELIZABETH II   Margaret
(1926 –)   (1930 –)

m
Philip
(1921 –)

Charles   Anne   Andrew   Edward
Prince of Wales (1950 –)   (1960 –)   (1964 –)
(1948 –)

m
Lady Diana Spencer
(1961 –)

William   Henry
(1982 –)   (1984 –)

The Royal Line
from Queen Victoria to the present day

Foreword

IT WAS DURING THE TOUR OF AUSTRALIA AND NEW ZEALAND BY PRINCE Charles, Princess Diana and the infant Prince William that my thoughts turned to compiling this book. A photograph of William wearing a romper suit evoked a memory of a picture of Prince Charles as a toddler wearing the same sort of garment, and from there it was only a few steps before I began thinking about the generations of babies born into the Royal Family. The more I delved into the subject the more fascinated I became with the stories attached to the births and the early childhood of the princes and princesses.

It seemed that the birth of Queen Victoria was the logical starting point. She was, in effect, the founder of the present monarchy and a major influence on the royalty of Europe as it was until the Second World War. Her mother's journey by jolting coach across Europe, with her father at the reins, so that Victoria would be born in England had its reward in the re-establishment and rehabilitation of the monarchy after an unhappy and uncertain period in the eighteenth and the early nineteenth centuries.

One of the enduring interests for me has been the differences seen in succeeding generations of royalty as far as their attitude to their children's upbringing is concerned. Victoria lent her name to an age of propriety and, for all her love of her family and her devotion to the family ethic, she is still remembered as a stern, and to some even frightening, matriarch. Following the death of her beloved Consort Albert in 1861 she rebuked her eldest daughter Victoria for failing to dress her baby (aged five months) in mourning.

The carefree, some thought careless, Edward and Alexandra, were followed by a return to stiffer values in the parenthood of George V and Queen Mary. The love and understanding afforded the present Queen and Princess Margaret during their babyhood has reaped benefits in the open family way in which the Queen and the Duke of

Edinburgh have brought up their children. It is tempting to wonder what Queen Victoria would have made of Prince William's first year.

In this book I have attempted to give some account of the often odd circumstances surrounding royal births (particularly those of the nineteenth century); the company in which these babies suddenly found themselves; their homes; their toys and the people (not always well chosen) who looked after them. It is intriguing to learn that it was an ancestor of Princess Diana who was called in to straighten out the chaos in Queen Victoria's nursery.

I have also retold some of the anecdotes, one or two, I have no doubt, embroidered over the years to the point of being apocryphal, which have grown up around these special childhoods. One of the major difficulties facing a chronicler of royal children is the bewildering collection of names given to them – few in total but so often repeated, and then replaced with a pet name or a secondary name as the recipient grew into adulthood. Victoria, Albert, Louise, Edward and George arise with confusing overlapping throughout the generations. Future historians will be pleased that Princess Margaret was given her name, and likewise Princess Anne, and that they, in turn, called their daughters Sarah and uniquely, Zara, thus breaking away from the long, familiar and yet confusing catalogue. Even the title Princess Diana, despite its widespread use, is strictly incorrect. Her true title is, in fact, simply the Princess of Wales.

One of the most rewarding aspects of this book for me has been the photographic research. This led me to the top of a turret at Windsor Castle, searching through the beautifully-bound family albums in the Royal Photographic Archives.

Turning these pages, I wondered how many times these endearingly personal photographs had been seen before. It is an added pleasure that I have been able to include some rarely published pictures in this book.

Chapter One

The Children of Queen Victoria

AT FOUR-THIRTY ON THE BLEAK MORNING OF 22 NOVEMBER 1840, SIX OF THE most eminent men in Britain were called from their beds. Their carriages were made ready and they drove to Buckingham Palace where, huddled together in a small panelled room, they were required to wait for several further hours. At two in the afternoon the event which had brought them hurrying through the dark night was accomplished – Queen Victoria gave birth to her first baby.

Lord Melbourne, the Prime Minister; Lord Palmerston, the Foreign Secretary; The Lord Chancellor; the Archbishop of Canterbury; the Bishop of London and the Comptroller of the Royal Household were required, by ancient custom, to be present at the birth of a prince or princess. In previous reigns there had always been the danger of, and rumours of, babies being exchanged in the cradle. Queen Victoria, however, refused to have the six men hovering around her bed 'to view our discomfort' and they were banished to a crowded ante-room, just a few yards away. When the child was delivered, it was brought to them at once for their detailed inspection.

Their conversations in this ante-room during those long, chilly and confined hours of waiting, must have touched at some time on the subject of whether the child would be a boy or a girl. Their wish, and the Queen's desire, was for a prince. In the event a girl, Victoria Adelaide Mary Louisa, was born. Her arrival was three weeks premature. Dr Locock, the obstetrician, is credited with the hollow phrase: 'Oh, Your Majesty, it's only a princess.' (Some historians do him the service of omitting the 'only' from this remark.) Queen Victoria, however, was as usual forthright in summing up the disappointment. 'Never mind, next time it will be a prince.'

Queen Victoria's father, the impoverished fourth son of George III, was fifty when he married. The sole legitimate heir of the unstable king,

Princess Charlotte, had died in childbirth – and the baby was stillborn.

The three remaining, unmarried sons of the king wed in haste in an attempt to produce an acceptable heir; a race won by the Duke of Kent who, in 1818, married Princess Victoire of Leiningen, a widow. From her German home she soon announced that she was expecting a baby.

The prospective father was taking no chances. He packed his pregnant wife and as many belongings as possible into a coach which he then *personally* drove across Europe, finally arriving at Dover. His child would be born on British soil. Their baby, Alexandrina Victoria was born on 24 May 1819. She was described as 'a princess plump and pretty as a partridge'. Eighteen years later she was woken by her mother at six o'clock one morning at Kensington Palace to discover that she was now the Queen of Great Britain.

In mid-November of 1840, the year of her marriage to her cousin Prince Albert, Victoria sent orders to the Royal upholsterers, Messrs. Seddon of Gray's Inn Road, London, for a cot and two baby baths to be designed and made.

The parents-to-be were both aged twenty-one. Prince Albert, as Victoria gratefully recorded in her diary, hardly left his wife's bedside during her confinement. If there was some little official disappointment that the new arrival was 'only a princess' then Albert did not share it. He delighted in his daughter, and his delight never waned. There was a strong bond between them, a relationship that the possessive queen sometimes showed signs of resenting in later years.

Because of the early arrival of the baby, arrangements at Buckingham Palace were woefully late and haphazard. The inexperience of the royal household in dealing with infants was quickly apparent. A room was hurriedly converted into a nursery on the first floor of the palace's remote north wing, a room that had previously been used by Victoria and Albert for breakfasting. Mrs Southey, the sister-in-law of the poet Robert Southey, was appointed Nursery Superintendent, not the best choice as it came to be seen.

One of the most extraordinary omissions attending the birth of the Queen's first child was that while it was taking place the selected wet nurse was comfortably at home in the Isle of Wight. Why someone from what was then a not infrequently inaccessible place to reach was chosen is a mystery. It seems even more of a mystery that the wet nurse should not be at hand as the time for the Queen's confinement approached. In the event a trusted page, Whiting, had to be hastily despatched to Southampton, and the nurse was roused from her bed to be rowed across the wide and wintry Solent in an open boat at the dead of night.

The christening of the Princess Royal on 10 February 1841 in the Chapel Royal, St James's Palace. It was the first anniversary of the marriage of Queen Victoria and the Prince Consort.

Nor was the location of the nursery ideal. Messrs. Seddon's gilt and silken cot was installed, as were the baths, but the jovial Albert, tiring of the long journeys from one end of the unwieldy palace to the other, was soon seen pulling the gurgling child along the unending corridors in a wickerwork basket.

On 10 February 1841, the first wedding anniversary of the Queen and her Consort, the three-month old princess was christened in the Chapel Royal, St James's Palace. She was given the names Victoria Adelaide Mary Louisa. To her loving parents she was 'Pussy'.

Watched by the élite of the nation the baby behaved with great aplomb, gazing at the uniforms, decorations and lights, with patent fascination. At no time did she cry but emitted a steady chuckle when the Archbishop touched her forehead with the holy water from the silver-gilt lily font her father had designed. She wore a gown of lace made by the women of Honiton in Devon. Lord Melbourne told the Queen that he truly believed the child was quite aware that all the fuss and ceremony was directed at her and no one else.

Thirty dozen bottles of mulled claret were poured into the gold punchbowl brought from Windsor Castle and used to toast the baby's name at the celebrations. The figure of Britannia, borne on Neptune's chariot, topped the christening cake. Carried aloft in her arms was a little figure of the baby Princess Royal. The toasts drunk that night were echoed throughout the kingdom and the world. But by that time Princess Pussy was asleep.

It is one of the happy quirks of history that a well-loved forebear of the present Princess of Wales featured in the everyday lives of these royal babies. Sarah Spencer, Lady Lyttelton, was a strong, sensible and humorous widow. A daughter of the second Earl Spencer she had five children of her own, and was a favourite lady-in-waiting of Queen Victoria. At Prince Albert's insistence, she was brought into Buckingham Palace to 'save the royal nursery' when it became apparent that the Princess Royal was not thriving as she should.

In the autumn of 1841 Queen Victoria was again pregnant and confessed herself to being 'low and depressed'. It was not merely what she considered to be her unpalatable state, but the fact that the little Princess Royal, after a healthy start to life, was sick and ailing. Prince Albert, beside himself with worry, called in Sir James Clark, the Royal Physician. The baby was unable to digest food and was losing weight. The august doctor prescribed a diet of asses' milk, chicken broth and 'drops of Calomel'.

Princess Pussy, with the Queen's new pregnancy, had become a little remote from her mother and it was Albert who had become alarmed at

Queen Victoria as a young girl.

the child's continuing decline. The asses' milk and the chicken broth were having no noticeable effect and in a fit of wrath he accused the hapless Sir James Clark of trying to poison the baby with the wretched drops of Calomel. The practical prince soon realised that the whole nursery arrangements were farcical. Mrs Southey was sent packing as was Lady Charlotte Finch, who also had charge of the royal infant. But the prime target of Albert's wrath was Baroness Lehzen, Queen Victoria's own governess, who haunted the nursery and in Albert's eyes had much to do with the state of affairs there. Because of her powerful influence on the Queen he had never liked her and now, in this clean sweep, he saw his chance to dispose of her, too. Her gossip, her intrigues and her hold over the Queen had, he considered, gone on far too long.

Victoria herself put up a stout resistance for the Baroness had been with her almost daily since she was five-years old, but her Consort could be as tough and singleminded as she. They had one of their rare quarrels, terminating in Albert's warning that unless the situation in the nursery was completely altered 'I shall have nothing more to do with it. Take the child away, do what you like – if she dies, you will have it on your conscience.'

The Queen surrendered. The Baroness went quietly away, early one morning, without saying goodbye to Victoria, but with her dignity intact and a handsome pension of £800-a-year.

The Queen corresponded with the Baroness throughout the rest of her life and when, one day in 1858, Victoria and Albert were visiting the Continent their train went through Bückburg, where she lived, she was on the platform to wave a sad handkerchief.

In March 1842, Lady Lyttelton was approached and asked to take charge of the royal nursery. She accepted and took over the position in the following month. Her verdict on the baby Princess Royal was that she had been over-watched and over-doctored. Within weeks Princess Pussy was again smiling and eating. By that time there was another baby in the nursery.

On 9 November 1841, at 10.48 in the morning at Buckingham Palace, the most momentous event in seventy-nine years of royal history in Britain took place – the birth of a male heir to the throne.

Prince Albert Edward, after several false alarms, set off by the Queen's previous premature birth, was born on Lord Mayor's Day, a London holiday, which was seen as a particularly good omen. Mrs Lilly, Her Majesty's nurse, who received a reward of £100 at each royal confinement, sent for the obstetrician, Dr Locock, in the early hours of the morning, and he arrived to deliver a 'fine large boy'.

The event, happening on this Cockney holiday, offered additional reasons for rejoicing. Throughout London Dr Locock's somewhat

Princess Alice guarded in her cradle by the Dandie Dinmont. Landseer's painting was carried out in secret as a surprise birthday present for Queen Victoria.

prosaic summing up was embroidered and *The Times* pronounced it as 'one universal feeling of joy'. *Punch* found verse to match the occasion:

> *Huzza, we've a little Prince at last!*
> *A roaring Royal boy!*
> *And all day long the booming bells,*
> *Have rung their peels of joy.*

A roaring Royal boy was a misjudgement. In the event Albert Edward was a dull child, his roaring attributed to attacks of rage. He was overshadowed in the nursery by his ebullient, intelligent, sister, and he was slow to walk and talk. His parents, with either a lack of poetry or lack of confidence in their ability to produce another prince, simply called him 'The Boy' and later 'Bertie'. He was described as a handsome baby with a pretty but somewhat large nose. He had grey-blue eyes and an attractive mouth. On 25 January 1842, just prior to the revolution in the palace nursery, he was christened at St George's Chapel, Windsor.

The interconnections of European royalty at that time were very evident at the christening. Crowns shone in the light. King Frederick William IV of Prussia was the chief godfather, and the Tsar of Russia and Louis Philippe of France, stood with him. The child was christened Albert Edward, Edward, after Victoria's father, and Albert after the Prince Consort. Fifty-nine years later he abandoned his first name and became King Edward VII of England.

It has to be said that Queen Victoria, allied to her feeling 'like a cow or a dog' during pregnancy, was also not entranced with small babies. She found them 'quite repulsive' until they reached the age of three or four months when, she judged, they were 'less froglike in movement and more human .

In contrast the amiable Prince Albert wrote: 'There is certainly a great charm as well as deep interest in watching the development of feelings and faculties in a little child, and nothing is more instructive for the knowledge of our own nature than to observe in a little creature the stages of development which, when we ourselves were passing through them, seemed scarcely to have an existence for us. I feel this daily in watching our young offspring whose characters are quite different and who show many lovable qualities.'

With her first child the Queen's attitude had been one of somewhat remote benevolence. It was six weeks before she saw Victoria, the Princess Royal, occupying the bath which Messrs. Seddon had made to her orders. Visits were officially confined to two periods a day and Victoria referred to the baby as 'quite a little toy for us'.

With the arrival of the second child, however, the Queen's attitude

Queen Victoria's first children, the Prince of Wales and the Princess Royal. Albert Edward was the first male heir to the throne to be born in seventy-nine years. Described as being a dull child, he was overshadowed in the nursery and the schoolroom by his lively older sister.

Sir W.C. Ross, R.A.
Min: Painter to the Queen.

Engraved by H. Robinson.

*Osborne House, Isle of
Wight, in August 1851.
Queen Victoria and Prince
Albert purchased the house
for £26,000. It was, wrote
Victoria, 'My little paradise'.*

changed noticeably. She spent more time in the nursery, sketching the babies and playing games.

By early 1843 Lady Lyttelton was helping the Queen to sort through baby clothes and linen left over from the first two children for she was expecting another child in April. Her frugality was ever a curious trait and clothes were expected to be passed from one infant to another as they were in normal families. (Indeed, it was said, that later when the family began to spend more time in Scotland, Victoria was delighted with Highland clothes because they could be of service to both boys and girls.)

The Honiton lace christening gown was brought out again for the christening of the second daughter, Alice Maud Mary, who was born on 25 April 1843. She was known to her parents as Fat Alice, or occasionally Fatima. Her second brother soon followed on 6 August 1844, when Alfred Ernest Albert (called 'Affie') was born. The Queen had four children under four years of age.

Victoria and Albert now decided that they must have a separate 'home' where they could be together as a real family. Buckingham Palace, with its archaic rooms and corridors, with the nursery so remote from the royal living quarters, would have to be supplemented. There were large gardens and grounds, of course, but Victoria and her Consort knew that here they were never far from the affairs of state and the demands of society. Windsor, although an improvement, was scarcely private. There were no secret gardens there, only grounds, and it was near enough London for the Queen to be available for duties she would have sometimes preferred to avoid.

As a girl, Victoria had visited the Isle of Wight with her mother and she had pleasant memories of this place. Situated off the South Coast, it was not too tiring a journey from London, but, because of the wide channel formed by the Solent, it was commendably remote. It was here that the royal couple found Osborne House and purchased it.

To visit Osborne today is to feel some of that happiness. The house, hugely enlarged into an Italianate mansion by the design of Albert himself, overlooks the splendid Osborne Bay which the Consort had likened (if over-enthusiastically) to the Bay of Naples.

It is, however, the touching and intimate things which bring to the visitor a little of the contentment that the royal family knew in those years: the children's gardening tools and wheelbarrows (each with the owner's initials) standing in a small shed in the garden which they themselves tended; the Swiss cottage, a wooden chalet imported in sections, with the interior scaled down to child-like proportions. The cottage was Prince Albert's idea of giving his children some notion of the normal proportions of life and how ordinary people lived. Albert

A portrait of Prince Alfred by Winterhalter. 'Affie', as he was known, was the Queen's second son, born in 1844.

Queen Victoria and Prince Albert with their five eldest children painted by Winterhalter in 1846. The children are (left to right) Prince Alfred, the Prince of Wales, Princess Alice, the baby Helena and the Princess Royal. At this time the couple had been married six years.

and Victoria delighted in having tea there as prepared by their offspring. Then there was the bathing machine which would trundle to the water when Her Majesty went for a dip in the sea, watched by her small and impressed brood, who delighted in the moment when only the royal head could be seen afloat.

The children's chairs and tables are still there, and the model fort called Prince Albert's Barracks bears a plaque saying: 'The bricks of the building were made by the children of Queen Victoria.' There is the famous and impressive painting by Winterhalter entitled 'The First of May' in which Victoria's seventh child, Prince Arthur, 'the little soldier', is seen exchanging birthday gifts with his godfather, the Duke of Wellington. Prince Arthur, who loved guns, swords and the stories of battles as told by the Duke, spent many happy hours in this fort.

Perhaps the most poignant, some would say eerie, memory of those far-off days of childhood at Osborne, however, is provided by the delicate plaster casts of the chubby feet and hands of the princes and princesses. They are displayed in the house, lying beside each other on velvet cushions.

Although Osborne today looks an impressive house, standing with its thousand acres falling away to the Solent, it was bought in 1845 for £26,000 as a small house from Lady Isabella Blanchard. The original building was demolished and Thomas Cubitt, the London builder, was commissioned to replace it. The Pavilion Wing, which was always the family's private home, had low ceilings and cosy rooms which the children and their parents enjoyed after the impersonal vastness of Buckingham Palace. The rebuilding of this wing took only a year to complete and the royal family was able to move in the autumn of 1846. They lived, however, for a further six years among the builder's materials as the rest of the house was completed.

This 'place of our own, quiet and retired' was not quite perfect until all the building work was complete. As Lady Lyttelton recorded in her diary: 'I have been out on a pleasant stroll about the brick and mortar heaps and then into the lower garden. There I saw the children burst out of the house after tea, in great joy.'

Once they had settled at Osborne the Queen made sure that they were there as often as possible. 'The children dine and tea in the garden and run about to their hearts' content', the Honourable Eleanor Stanley, a maid of honour, noted in July 1848. The whole royal family, she reported, 'children, Queen and all seem to be out the whole day long'. Victoria confessed that she only gave the minimum time possible to signing documents and other matters of State and that she had scarcely bothered to read a book for weeks. Outings were arranged to different parts of the Isle of Wight and to the mainland, which was always visible, but not always accessible across the water.

ABOVE: *Princess Helena and Louise ride a mule in 1854.* BELOW: *The nursery at Osborne House.*

But it was the intimate family atmosphere that the children and their parents so much enjoyed. Eleanor Stanley noted: 'The children went to their garden to eat gooseberries and strawberries – at least the few that the squirrels had left.'

In the green island, with the comforting sight of the ships of the British navy sliding through the channel on one side, the easy hills rising on the other, evenings were spent all together in the simple sitting room. Victoria and Albert with their infant family had discovered what the Queen called 'my little paradise'.

The four eldest children, supervised in the royal nursery by Lady Lyttelton, known to them as 'Laddle', were of differing temperaments and abilities. Poor Bertie, as Albert Edward was known, was overshadowed by his siblings in almost everything. He was a sadly dull child, slow to learn, slow to grow, so that even the younger children outdistanced him, and his elder sister, with whom he was inclined to fight, took a delight in scoring off him.

Lady Lyttelton had advanced views on controlling the nursery. Even though she had been known to administer a beating she recorded: 'They wear out so soon and one is never sure they are fully understood by the child as belonging to the naughtiness.' She believed that the alternative action of the loss of a treat, being sent to bed without supper, or being forbidden to go for a walk with their parents, had a greater effect.

Alice, the second daughter, despite her unfortunate appellation of Fat Alice, proved to be one of the liveliest and most interesting of Victoria's brood. There is a fetching portrait by Sir Edwin Landseer of her as a baby asleep in a carved cradle guarded by her dog, a Dandie Dinmont, keeping a suspicious eye on the artist, who had to work in secret. Prince Albert would arrange for Landseer to be smuggled into the palace to paint the picture which was presented as a surprise gift to Victoria on her birthday.

Alice died in her thirties, in 1878, while nursing her children through diphtheria. When her daughter, Princess Victoria of Battenberg, went to Windsor for the birth of her first baby in February 1885, she lay in the same bed in which both she and her mother had been born. Queen Victoria sat beside her bed, holding her hand just as she had held the hand of Alice, her mother twenty two years earlier. The new baby, also named Alice, was the mother of Prince Philip, Duke of Edinburgh.

When Alfred, who was born at Windsor Castle on 6 August 1844, was two weeks old, his father, who still had strong ties with his homeland, wrote to his brother, Ernest, who had produced no heir: 'The little one shall from his youth be taught to love the dear, small, country to which

Winterhalter's famous painting 'The First of May'. It was Prince Arthur's first birthday and the eighty-second birthday of his godfather, the Duke of Wellington, after whom he was named.

ABOVE: *Little drummer boy. Arthur, the soldier prince.* OPPOSITE ABOVE: *Beatrice, aged one, in pony carriage with Leopold (on tailboard) and Arthur at Osborne, 1858.* OPPOSITE BELOW: *Leopold, Queen Victoria's eighth child aged four years.*

ABOVE: *Mrs Thurston, the nanny, holding Louise in 1848. (Left to right) Albert Edward, Helena, Alice, Victoria and Alfred.* BELOW: *Arthur, Helena and Louise photographed in fancy dress at Windsor in 1856.*

ABOVE: *Osborne, 1857. (Left to right) Alfred, Prince Albert, Helena, Alice, Arthur, Queen Victoria holding Beatrice, Victoria, Louise, Leopold and Albert Edward.* BELOW: *Beatrice on her second birthday.*

he belongs in every respect, as does his papa.' The promise was fulfilled when Alfred was given the title Duke of Coburg.

Alfred was ever a contented baby, good-tempered and peaceful amid the frequent tumult caused by the nursery rivalries of his older brother and sisters. He was the one who sat watching quietly when the toys were flying.

As Victoria's infants arrived regularly, so they benefited, or perhaps suffered, from some of the innovations of the century. Helena Augusta Victoria (known as Lenchen), born on 25 May 1846, had some of the glory stolen from her at her christening by the installation of gas lighting in the chapel at Buckingham Palace. As the gas jets whirred and sizzled, so the eyes of the assembled nobility were on them and not on the baby who cried at the font.

Leopold, born on 7 April 1853, was delivered with the aid of anaesthetic – chloroform – much to Victoria's relief. Victoria, who had always hated the ordeal of labour, welcomed the innovation. A half-teaspoon of chloroform was poured onto a handkerchief which was then rolled into a funnel, the open end being placed on the Queen's mouth. The dose was repeated after ten minutes.

'Dr Snow gave that blessed chloroform and the effect was soothing, quieting and delightful beyond measure,' wrote the Queen.

Traditionalists, naturally, were disposed to blame the revolutionary anaesthetic used at Leopold's birth for the fact that he was always the sickly one of the family – in fact he suffered from *haemophilia*, the blood disease. Little Leo, or Poor Little Leo, had to be kept apart from his boisterous brothers and sisters for the slightest knock could start a haemorrhage. His mother's recollection, however, was uncharitable. At four years of age, she had this opinion: 'He is tall but holds himself worse than ever and is a very common looking child, very plain in face, clever but an oddity and not an engaging child, though amusing.' Poor little Leo indeed!

Between the christening of Helena by gaslight and the delivery of Leopold by chloroform, a space of only seven years, two further children were born to the Queen. Lady Lyttelton, recording the arrival of Louise Caroline Alberta (named after Albert's mother) on 18 March 1848, wrote: 'Our new baby is right Royal. Very large, extremely fair with white satin hair, large blue eyes and regular features, a most perfect child from head to foot.' Sadly the beloved, but firm, Laddle, now left the Palace, after eight years in the nursery, to care for her grandchildren after the death of her own daughter.

Arthur, who became Duke of Connaught, was born on 1 May 1850, the eighty-first birthday of the Duke of Wellington, who became his godfather. How much this birthday influenced him in later years it is difficult to tell but from childhood he was heard to pronounce: 'Arta is

Beatrice, Queen Victoria's youngest child. When she was four years old her father died and she became her mother's closest companion.

going to be a soldier.' He was happiest at Osborne manning the battlements of Albert Barracks, and in later life delighted in manoeuvres and parades.

Victoria and her Consort had been married for seventeen years when their ninth and last child, Beatrice May Victoria Feodore was born on 14 April 1857. This time the Queen was all-approving. 'The flower of our flock', was the endorsement, while Albert wrote to his friend Baron Stockmar: 'Little Beatrice is an extremely attractive, pretty, intelligent child. Indeed the most amusing baby we have.'

When Beatrice was only four, Albert died of typhoid fever. The grief of Victoria was overwhelming and it was this last princess who gave her most comfort. As she grew she became her mother's constant companion, so much so that Victoria could not bear the thought of her leaving England to marry Prince Henry of Battenberg in 1884. She only gave her consent on the condition that the prince forsook his own country and lived in England, which he did.

In her long reign Queen Victoria, who had brought prestige back to the British monarchy, had influenced the lives of generations of royal children. She had given birth to her first child in 1840 and had lived to hold the baby who a century later was to reign as George VI. Her children and their children had married into most of the reigning houses of Europe. She was indeed the grandmother of European Royalty.

Chapter Two

The Children of King Edward VII

AMONG THE ROYAL FAMILIES OF EUROPE THERE EXISTED A MARRIAGE MARKET which, ever mindful of religion and breeding, arranged unions between suitable partners. There were strict stratas of allowable unions and, of course, it was limited by the boundaries of the candidates' backgrounds. Many of the marriages of British royalty in the early nineteenth century had involved German princes or princesses, and it was therefore with something like relief that the British people heard in 1862 that their future queen was to be from Denmark.

It was decided that the time had come for the pleasure-loving Edward, Prince of Wales, to take a wife, although he was less enthusiastic, enjoying the status of being a single man (something which marriage did not, as it happened, unduly disrupt). His sister, Princess Victoria, was despatched to Strelitz, in Germany in the May of 1861, and her report in a letter to her mother of how she found the eligible Alexandra, the seventeen-year-old daughter of Prince and Princess Christian of Denmark, settled Edward's future.

'She is,' wrote the princess, 'a good deal taller than I am, has a lovely figure but very thin, a complexion as beautiful as possible . . . very fine, white, regular teeth, and very fine large eyes, with extremely prettily marked eyebrows . . . a very fine, well-shaped nose, very narrow but a little long . . . her whole face is very narrow, her forehead too but well-shaped and not at all flat. Her voice, her walk, carriage and manner are perfect. She is one of the most ladylike and aristocratic looking people I ever saw. She is as simple and natural and unaffected as possible . . . and seems exceedingly well brought up.'

Even with the evidence of a dossier like this, Edward was reluctant to marry. In September 1861 the couple met for the first time at a supposedly chance encounter at Speyer Cathedral near Baden, which had been engineered by the various interested parties. Three months later Prince Albert, the beloved Consort, died, so it was not until

September 1862 that the couple's betrothal was finally announced.

Queen Victoria, although anxious for the wedding to take place because it was 'a thing that Papa was most anxious for', decided that the ceremony should be properly muted in view of the official mourning still taking place for her Consort. It was, therefore, announced that the marriage would not take place in London, but at St George's Chapel, Windsor, a decision which was almost universally unpopular. Londoners, who loved royal events and particularly weddings, felt they had been cheated. *Punch* suggested derisively that as the affair was to take place in an obscure Berkshire village, noted only for an aged castle with no sanitary arrangements (the notorious drains of Windsor Castle having been, it was rumoured, the cause of the Prince Consort's death from typhoid) the only notice which should appear in *The Times* should read: 'On the 10th. Inst. by Dr Longley, assisted by Dr Thomson, Albert Edward England, K.G. to Alexandra Denmark. No cards.'

Londoners made the best of things by greeting the princess at Gravesend where she arrived in the royal yacht, on the 8 March 1863, three days before the wedding. The route to the station was festooned with evergreens and orange blossom, and the barns and buildings beside the Kentish railway line were hung with loyal banners.

If the wedding was subdued, then the birth of the couple's first child was even more unostentatious. January of 1864 was in the middle of a bone-hard winter with deep snow and thick frost. Alexandra's baby was expected in March and at the end of the first week in the New Year she spent a day watching skating on the lake at Frogmore, the royal house near Windsor. On the following day, wrapped warmly in blankets and sitting in a sledge on the ice, she watched her sporty husband take part in an ice hockey match at Virginia Water. That evening, at Frogmore, she complained of feeling ill and her lady-in-waiting, Lady Macclesfield, the mother of thirteen children, recognized the signs. She sent for the local Windsor doctor, Dr Brown, who arrived in good time to deliver a baby boy, Prince Albert Victor, weighing only three-and-three-quarter pounds.

All arrangements for the birth had been made at Marlborough House but Lady Macclesfield was resourceful. She took herself to Caley's, the drapers of Windsor (still to be seen in the High Street), and her shopping list is still preserved in the royal archives: 'Outfit provided for his Royal Highness the Eldest Son of the Prince of Wales', says the document. 'Two yards of coarse flannel, six yards of superfine flannel, one sheet of wadding (lent by Mrs Knollys), one basket (contents wanting) and one superb lace Christening robe.'

The new arrival's first clothing, however, was provided by the torn-up petticoat of Lady Macclesfield. It was fortunate that Lord Granville was a house guest at Windsor and he was qualified to certify that the new prince was the genuine article. Six doctors hurried post haste from London, arriving hours after the birth. As they tumbled breathless into her room Princess Alexandra burst into peals of laughter.

As untimely as the baby's arrival might have been for those whose duty it was to be concerned with it, to the people and the press it gave the opportunity to prolong the seasonal celebrations. *The Times* welcomed this 'New Year's gift which the Princess has presented to the country', and *Punch* chose to mark the occasion with a Nursery Song with warlike overtones.

> *Oh, hush thee, my darling, thy sire is a Prince*
> *Whom Mama beheld skating not quite five hours since,*
> *And Grandpapa Christian is off to the fray,*
> *With the Germans who'd steal his nice Duchy away.*
>
> *But slumber, my darling, the English are true,*
> *And will help him for love of Mama and of you.*
> *The Channel Fleet's coming with powder and shot*
> *And the Germans must run, or they'll catch it all hot!*

The verses referred to hostilities between Prussia and Denmark which had been in progress for some time and had been a great anxiety to Princess Alexandra. Where the British sympathies lay is obvious, but what the many German relatives of the new child thought can only be conjectured. The Princess Royal, for example, whose glowing recommendation had brought Alexandra to England was married to Prince Frederick William of Prussia.

The American Ambassador, writing of the prince's premature arrival in his journal, summed up the general reaction thus: 'As the event was not expected for another two months and no preparations were made for it the public feeling is a mixture of agreeable disappointment and ill-suppressed risibility.'

Queen Victoria, attending the christening at St George's Chapel, Windsor, recorded that the baby kept up a 'steady roar' throughout the ceremony.

Prince Albert Victor Christian Edward – Eddy as he was called – turned out to be a slow but amiable child, a great favourite with his mother and sisters. His father was worried about his indolence but approved of his gentleness and good nature. However, his brother George, born on 3 June 1865, was quick to outstrip Eddy. A bright and intelligent spirit he easily dominated his elder brother. When the young princes played at 'Kings and Queens' with the children of the Duke and Duchess of Teck, it was the younger George who took over the role of monarch, with the

The wedding of the Prince of Wales and Princess Alexandra of Denmark in 1863 at St George's Chapel, Windsor. Queen Victoria, in deep mourning for Prince Albert, watches from Katharine of Aragon's closet.

OPPOSITE: *The Prince and Princess of Wales with their first child, Albert Victor, born in January 1864.*
ABOVE: *Family outing in 1864. (Left to right) Prince William of Prussia, Princess of Wales, Albert Victor, Beatrice and Queen Victoria.* RIGHT: *Albert Victor aged two. Small boys' clothes in Victorian times were often indistinguishable from their sisters'.*

toddler Princess May, becoming queen, strange but accurate playing of roles as events proved.

Prince George was born after his parents had returned from a Hallé Orchestra concert. The princess complained of weariness and quickly produced her baby, this time a month early. Writing to her uncle, the King of the Belgians, Queen Victoria remarked that the new prince was said to be 'nice and plump'.

Queen Victoria, however, was less than satisfied with the choice of names for the new arrival. She did not like the name George, since, she reminded the young parents sourly, the House of Hanover, to which the name belonged, had been a far from satisfactory line of kings. She wanted the child called Albert, 'since all dearest papa's descendants should bear the name' but Edward and Alexandra stuck to their choice and replied that George was an excellent name with an English ring about it. At the christening, at Windsor, the final choice was George Frederick Ernest Albert, but there was some consolation for the eternal widow that 'Windsor Uniform', frock coat with knee breeches and silk stockings, as designed by her late Prince Consort was *de rigeur*. The anthem was also composed by the ubiquitous Albert.

The pursed lips of Queen Victoria were often in evidence when the children of her eldest son were discussed. In her puritan fashion she disapproved of the busy and lighthearted social life which both Edward and his wife enjoyed. She believed that Alexandra's frail appearance resulted from this and warned the prince that he should take greater care of her. Nor did she hold much admiration for the way the boys were brought up, either physically or in their manners. The easy-going attitude of the parents, she believed, led to wilful behaviour on the part of the infants. To her credit she also liked to tell of the amusing things they did, especially George, who once behaved so badly at lunch that he was instructed by his father to go under the table as a punishment. This he did, emerging before all the guests having taken off his clothes.

The character of Prince Edward, the Prince of Wales, during the early years of his youth, during the babyhood of his children and later, as King Edward VII, has undergone much analysis. That he was a feckless husband there is no doubt. Much emphasis has been put on the strict education forced upon him when he was not capable of handling it, by his determined royal parents. It has even been said that his character, particularly his attitude to the devoted Alexandra, was that of a split personality.

In February of 1867, when expecting her third child, Alexandra waited impatient and ill in London, for the return of her husband from St Petersburg, where he had been attending the wedding of the

Chiswick House. In the 1870s the Wales children and their cousins, the Tecks, played in these grounds. The childhood game of 'Kings and Queens' was the beginning of an intriguing story.

ABOVE: *George in 1871.*
Although younger than
Albert Victor, he was the
dominant son of the Prince
of Wales. BELOW: *Princess*
Mary of Teck who
eventually became Queen
Mary, consort of George V.
OPPOSITE: *Prince George*
aged two. One of the unruly
Wales children, he once
emerged naked from under
the dinner table.

ABOVE: *Louise, described by Queen Victoria as a 'poor little baby with a cough'.* BELOW: *Louise, aged two, in May 1869.* OPPOSITE: *Albert Victor, George and Louise, the elder Wales children, pose with a large, shaggy and anonymous dog.*

Tsarevitch Alexander and, if the rumours were true, the ladies of the Russian court also.

Edward was away six weeks and had hardly returned when, on 15 February, despite his wife's obvious indisposition, he went racing and then on to dine at Windsor. The princess became much worse and three telegrams were sent asking Edward to return. He did not do so until the following day by which time the doctors had diagnosed rheumatic fever. Five days later their daughter was born.

Louise, who was named after her maternal grandmother, was described by Queen Victoria, as 'a poor little baby with a cough'. She had been born without the aid of anaesthetic. The mother's illness prevented its use and the Queen was very disturbed at the deterioration in her daughter-in-law's health. Edward, in the meantime, pursued his usual round of pleasure. Whatever the theories and perhaps the reasons for his callous behaviour, the fact remained that he was someone who seldom came home until the early hours.

Lady Macclesfield watched and noted with as much disapproval as Queen Victoria. She wrote in a letter: 'The Princess had another bad night chiefly owing to the Prince promising to come in at 1 a.m. and keeping her in a perpetual fret, refusing to take her opiate for fear she would be asleep when he came, and he never came in until 3 a.m.'

When, on 10 May, the baby was christened, the ceremony had to be held in the drawing room at Marlborough House, with the palely beautiful Alexandra in a wheeled chair. Queen Victoria concluded that the baby did not look very strong. She was a constant critic of the way her son and daughter-in-law brought up their children. She recorded a private theory that they were 'under-sized and pigeon breasted'. To the Princess Royal she wrote: 'The race will be a puny one which would have distressed dear Papa.' Three of Victoria's own children outlived all those of Edward and Alexandra.

Princess Louise was known in the household as 'Looloo', and her sister, Victoria born on 6 July 1868, as 'Toria'. The easy-going parents, and the tolerant régime in the nursery, had produced offspring who were different things to different observers. Lady Geraldine Somerset called Toria 'sharp, quick, merry and amusing'. But once again to the regal grandmother she was merely 'exceedingly naughty'. After one visit, the Queen summed them up thus: 'They are such ill-bred children I can't fancy them at all.' Even the patient Lady Somerset sighed: 'The boys are as wild as hawks and the princesses rampaging little girls.' They were, she sighed, past all management.

A third daughter, Maud, known as 'Harry' after her father's friend, Admiral Harry Keppel, was born on 26 November 1869. This new-comer to the nursery hardly diminished the unruliness of the royal roost, and Maud was described as being a tomboy.

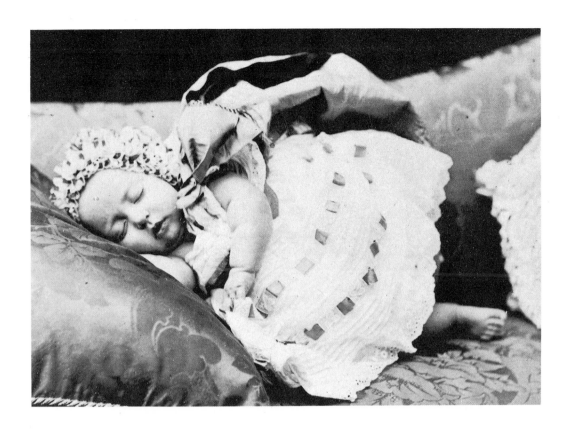

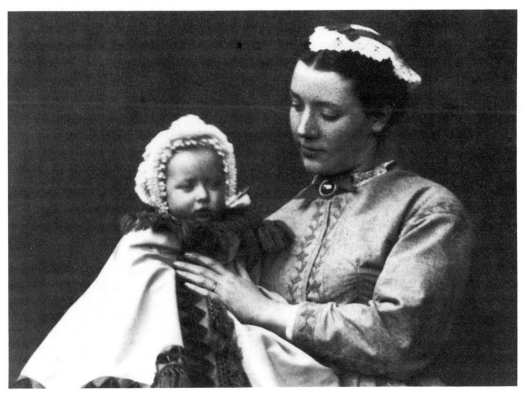

ABOVE: *Victoria, born in 1868. Queen Victoria described her as being 'exceedingly naughty'.* BELOW: *Victoria aged one with her nurse, Mrs Quinlan.*

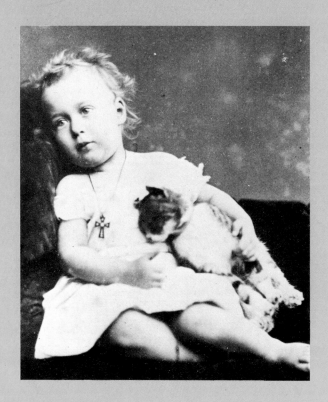

ABOVE: *The Wales children in 1870. After one visit, Queen Victoria noted: 'They are such ill-bred children I can't fancy them at all.'* LEFT: *Maud, the Wales' youngest child, aged two.* OPPOSITE: *Maud with the Princess of Wales. Maud was a tomboy nicknamed 'Harry' after her father's friend Harry Keppel.*

TOP TO BOTTOM: *Maud, George, Louise, Victoria and Albert Victor, photographed in 1871.*

The Prince of Wales did little to discourage the unorthodoxy of his offspring's upbringing. Returning from a visit to India, having been away nine months, he brought back with him a Himalayan bear, a large aviary of tropical birds, a family of monkeys and a miniature pony called Nawab. This was the favourite of the small children for it was small enough, and nimble enough, to mount the main staircase at Sandringham with one or more of them on its back.

It was at Sandringham in Norfolk that this rumbustious family felt most at home. The estate was purchased by Edward for an astonishing £220,000 in 1862. It consisted of Sandringham Hall, five farms, many cottages, some in a very poor state of repair, seven thousand acres of farmland, a two hundred acre park and a small stone church. It was a few miles from the south shore of the Wash, set in typically flat East Anglian countryside. The original house was not practical for the young royal couple and, at great expense, it was virtually rebuilt into a large solid red-brick mansion complete with billiard room and what was called an American indoor bowling alley.

It was here that Alexandra, the daughter of not-very-rich parents from a small country, could lead the life she loved and be with the children she, and her husband, so much indulged. She had six children in seven years, four being under six years of age when Princess Maud was born.

Social life went on unabated, with exciting house parties in Marlborough House, their London home, and at Sandringham. These gatherings, at which the small princes and princesses mingled with the guests, sometimes lasted for days. One party might be from Monday to Thursday with a week-end party taking from Friday to Sunday. The children delighted in the constant changing of guests and there were always practical jokes to add to the entertainment. Cakes of soap were served as cheese, with the little perpetrators stifling their giggles as the victim bit deeply. Then there was always Uncle Affie, a natural target, who might find the pockets of his evening clothes stuffed with sweets.

On one occasion the Himalayan bear was released from its pit so that it roamed the grounds to the enchantment of the children and the fright of grown ups. The monkeys not infrequently found themselves free to cause havoc in the house, and once a cockerel was introduced into a bedroom to startle the sleeping occupants with its crowing. The children's boisterous spirits were a by-word in society.

No one was safe from the pranksters. Disraeli, sitting at a dinner party one evening, was astonished to find his trouser legs being tugged and looked below the table to see the diminutive face of a princess who had crawled between the many feet to play the joke on him. And yet Alexandra hardly seemed to notice, and certainly rarely chastised them for their outrageous behaviour.

There was an endearing story at the time that Alexandra had ordered the carpenters to cut a hole in the floor of the nursery, which was situated at the top of the house, so that a sleeping infant could be lowered in a tray-like device for a goodnight kiss without being woken.

The easy-going attitude that Alexandra and Edward adopted towards their children did not however allow them to be anything but polite and considerate to the servants, one of the few things about their parental methods that Queen Victoria thought praiseworthy. Charles Fuller, the nursery footman who attended the small princes, was a great favourite. Edward and Alexandra's doting did not extend to much expenditure on toys and Fuller's skill at making wooden playthings, ships, spinning tops, toy soldiers, came in very useful.

Alexandra had become somewhat deaf, which doubtless aided her indulgence towards her rowdy brood. It might also be said that her attitude to her husband's not infrequent romantic wanderings was much the same. She loved both Edward and her family.

She was not, in fact, an intellectual person. The product of a happy childhood she lingered in its protection long after she herself had become a mother. Her endearments and often her conversation were baby-like, causing her to write to her son George: 'A big kiss for your lovely little face.' He was then the bearded captain of a warship. He, however, responded to her mood by signing himself 'Your loving little Georgie'. Sometimes the princess would, in her childlike simplicity, send presents to young adults that were suitable only for children. On her daughter's nineteenth birthday the poor young lady had to sit through an infant's tea-party.

There came one tragedy into their carefree world. On 6 April 1871, Alexandra gave birth to her final child, a boy, Alexander John Charles Albert. It was another premature birth and, as usual, nothing was ready. There were no baby clothes and no wet nurse. The baby lived only twenty-four hours. Edward himself, shaking with tears, placed the small body in the white coffin and with his two small sons walked to the little churchyard at Sandringham for the burial. Alexandra overwhelmed with grief, watched from her bedroom window as the woeful little procession left the house.

Of the other five children, Maud became Queen of Norway, Louise became Princess Royal in 1905, and Victoria remained unmarried, being her mother's constant and devoted companion throughout her life.

As for the two boys, Albert and George, who had played at coronations as children with Princess May of Teck, at Chiswick House, fate played a strange hand. Albert, the heir to the throne, died six weeks before he and Princess May were to marry in February 1892. His younger brother George married her instead. They became King George V and Queen Mary. The childhood game had come true.

Chapter Three

The Children of King George V

AFTER THE EASY-GOING MANNER OF HIS UPBRINGING BY EDWARD AND Alexandra, it is surprising that the man who was to become King George V ruled his own children with stentorian voice and strict rules. He always thought of himself as a sailor (his study was fitted out like a captain's cabin and his first action each morning was to tap the barometer), and even his youngest offspring were expected to behave as though they were part of the crew.

Princess Mary, his wife, although of gentler disposition remained in royal awe of Prince George. The children, she believed, '. . . must realise that not only is he their father, but he will one day be their King'. She, even more so than Queen Victoria, who was still on the throne, had a puzzled, almost aloof relationship with her infants, as if she did not quite know what to do with them. When her husband was absent, however, she tried hard to fashion some sort of motherly pact. Although her report about the infant Prince Edward in a letter to her husband might have been better phrased, the pathetic uncertainty is apparent. 'Baby was delicious at tea this evening,' she wrote. 'He is in a charming frame of mind and I hope he will be when you return tomorrow. He often calls for Papa and seems to miss you very much. I really believe he begins to like me at last, he is most civil to me.'

Prince George and Princess Mary were married in July 1893, a year after the death from pneumonia of Albert Victor. He died only six weeks before he was due to marry his childhood playmate – Princess Mary.

Princess Mary's names were in fact Victoria Mary Augusta Louise Olga Pauline Claudine Agnes, but despite this caravan she was known within the family simply as May – because her mother called her 'My Mayflower'. She was born in May of 1867 to Francis, Duke of Teck and Princess Mary Adelaide. Her mother was 33-years old and Mary was her first child. Her parents enjoyed London society to the full and Mary

Adelaide, a large and jolly woman, was very popular. She was known widely and affectionately as Fat Mary.

At the christening of her daugher at Kensington Palace it was said that the Archbishop of Canterbury recited the baby's eight Christian names like a litany and then drew a deep breath. The Duke, an amiable man with little to occupy him, spent his time re-organizing the garden and the disposition of the furniture at White Lodge, Richmond. Almost every week saw some new arrangement within the house and Princess Mary's governess, Madame Helene Bricka, recorded that whenever she returned from an absence even of a few days, her entire quarters might well have been re-organized. This apparently did not incommode her particularly since she remained with the family for many years, eventually becoming governess to the children of Princess Mary and Prince George.

Mary was clever but reserved; a quietness, a gentle aloofness she kept all her life. She shared Queen Victoria's distaste of pregnancy and childbirth. She considered it 'boring'.

When, in the hot summer of 1894, Princess Mary was about to give birth to her first child, she asked her doctors if she could go from Buckingham Palace to White Lodge, her parents' home in the airy spaces of Richmond Park. There a son, who became eventually, and briefly, King Edward VIII was born. His father wrote in his diary for 23 June 1894: 'At ten a sweet little boy was born and weighed eight pounds. Mr Asquith, the Home Secretary, came to see him.'

It was Ascot week and the child's ever-socializing grandfather, Edward, Prince of Wales, was at a ball in the Fishing Temple at Virginia Water. He silenced the orchestra in mid-tune and called for the dancing to cease. 'It is with pleasure,' he announced loudly, 'that I am able to inform you of the birth of a son to the Duke and Duchess of York – I propose a toast to the young prince!'

At that moment, for the first time in history, there were living in England three princes who were in direct line to the throne. But still ruling the nation was the indomitable Queen Victoria.

The redoubtable monarch, however, was apparently less impressed than the newspapers and the country in general, at the availability of three possible kings. Writing to the Empress Frederick of Prussia – her own daughter Vicky – she observed: 'It seems that it has never happened in this country that there should be three direct heirs and the Sovereign alive . . . but although it is a great pleasure and satisfaction it is not such a marvel . . .' Then, referring to a proposal made by the now-dead Albert Victor to her granddaughter Alix, which was answered in the negative, she wrote: '. . . if Alicky had not refused Eddy in '89 I might have had a great grandchild four years ago already.' (Alicky the

*The wedding of Prince
George and Princess Mary
of Teck at St James's
Palace on 6 July 1893.
Mary was to have married
George's brother, Albert
Victor, but he died shortly
before the wedding was to
take place in 1892.*

Edward, the first child of Prince George and Princess Mary, born at White Lodge, Richmond in 1894. He became King Edward VIII but reigned for less than one year before abdicating in December 1936.

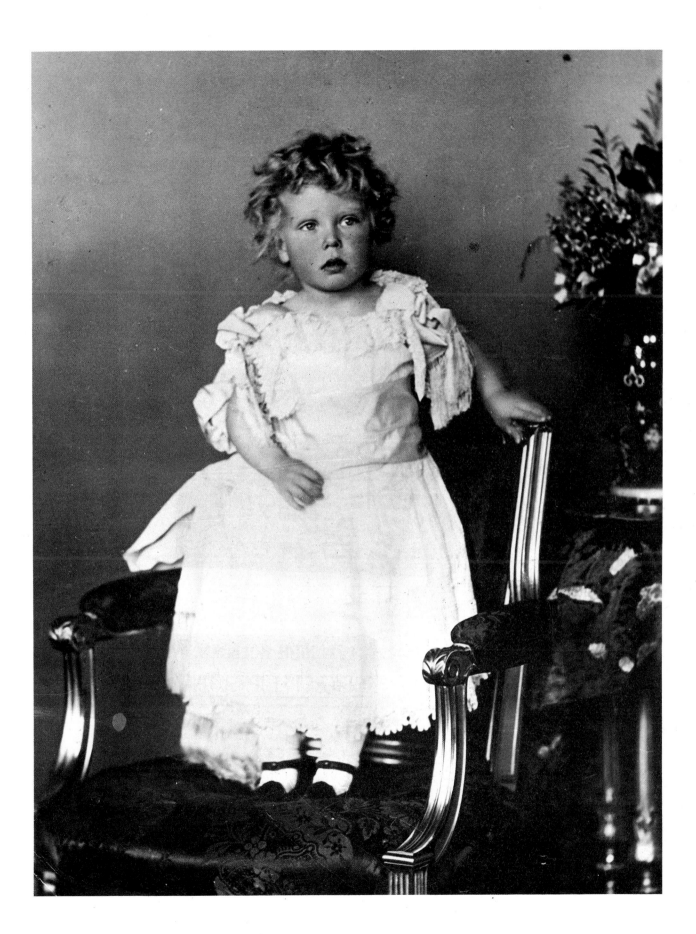

Queen Victoria with her great-grandson Edward. He called her 'Gangan'.

daughter of Princess Alice became instead the wife of Nicolas, Tsar of Russia. They and their children were executed by Bolshevik revolutionaries in 1918.)

The seventy-five year-old Queen was excited and pleased enough, however, to take the short train journey from Windsor to Richmond four days later to see the new prince. Throngs of happy subjects cheered her carriage from the station. A marquee had been erected on the lawn of White Lodge and in one day fifteen hundred people had queued to put their names in the visitors' book as a sign of loyalty and congratulation.

'I went yesterday,' Victoria recorded, 'with Beatrice, Nicky, Alicky, etc. to see May and the baby who is a very fine strong boy, a pretty child. May, I did not see as it was rather too soon and the doctor especially wished that she should be kept very quiet; but she is perfectly well and Dr Williams said one could not be a stronger and healthier parent than she is, which is a great thing for the future.'

Prophecies were already being piled on the unsuspecting prince's head. While names for the baby were being discussed the Marchioness of Waterford, a close friend of Queen Victoria, sent a message from her deathbed reminding Her Majesty of a prophecy that a King David would rule the earth. The chosen names were Edward (after his father's deceased brother) Albert (naturally) followed by Christian (after his grandmother's Danish father) followed by George Andrew Patrick David, representing the patron saints of the four countries of Great Britain.

To look at the list of guests and godparents at the child's christening in the drawing room at White Lodge, on 16 July 1894, is to read a roll-call of a vanished age. The twelve godparents included the Tsarevich, the King and Queen of Denmark, the Queen of the Hellenes, King William of Württemberg and the Duke of Saxe-Coburg-Gotha.

All the slow pomp of such occasions was observed and it was left to the great-grandmother, Victoria the indefatigable diarist and letter writer, to make her criticism and record intimate moments. 'The dear, fine baby wearing the Honiton lace robe (made for Vicky's Christening and worn by all our children and my English grandchildren) was brought in and handed to me. I then gave him to the Archbishop and received him back. The child was very good. There was an absence of all music, which I thought was a pity.' The heat of the crowded room proved too much for the elderly monarch and she retired for a few private minutes. 'When the service was over I went with May to the Long Gallery where in '61 I used to sit with Dearest Albert and look through dear Mama's letters. Had tea with May and afterwards we were photographed, I holding the baby on my lap, Bertie and Georgie standing behind me, thus making the four generations.'

Edward, always known as David, did not grow up to rule the earth. He ruled Great Britain and her Empire for less than a year before abdicating on 11 December 1936 to marry Wallis Simpson, the American divorcee.

With hindsight, there is the sound of a knell in *The Times* leading article of 25 June 1894, concerning the birth of the boy. 'The young prince,' it said, 'is heir to a noble inheritance . . . to a station of unequalled dignity, but more than all to the affection of a loyal people, which it will be his office to keep and to make his own, our heartfelt prayer is that he may prove worthy of so great a trust.'

When Prince Edward's brother was born in 1895 there was much consternation over the date of his arrival. Known dolefully in the family as 'Mausoleum Day' 14 December was the double anniversary of the deaths of Prince Albert, the Consort, in 1861 and of his daughter Princess Alice in 1878. On that day it was the custom for Queen Victoria and her children to pray at the mausoleum at Frogmore where both were interred.

When the baby prince came into the world at that inopportune time, his father, Prince George wrote to the Queen: 'I am afraid, dear Grandmama, you were rather distressed that he was born on the fourteenth, that doubly sad day for you and all our family. Dear Grandmama, we propose, with your permission, to call him Albert after dear Grandpapa.'

Permission was, naturally, given and at the christening (postponed by another death, that of Prince Henry of Battenberg, husband of Victoria's youngest daughter Beatrice) he was given the names Albert Frederick Arthur George, but he was known to the family as 'Bertie'. When he became King in 1936, after his brother had given up the throne, he reigned as George VI.

The ceremony took place at the family church, St Mary's, Sandringham, for it was in Norfolk that Prince George and Princess Mary spent much time. They had been given York Cottage, as a wedding gift by the Prince of Wales. It was set in the grounds of Sandringham a short distance from the main house where Edward, Prince of Wales, and Alexandra were still in residence, and was originally constructed to take the overflow of guests from the heavily populated houseparties or as bachelor quarters.

'It was and remains a glum little villa,' was the description recalled by Harold Nicholson, 'encompassed by thickets of laurel and rhododendron, shadowed by huge wellingtonias and separated by an abrupt rim of lawn from a pond at the edge of which a leaden pelican gazed in dejection upon water lilies and bamboo . . .'

The house was constructed of local brown stone, rough-cast on the

Kings in infancy. Albert (left), who became George VI, and his elder brother Edward in their perambulators. A nurse mistreated the children until she was discovered, and dismissed, by their parents.

*York Cottage,
Sandringham. George and
Mary were happy here for
over thirty years. Harold
Nicholson described it as a
'glum little villa with
features indistinguishable
from those of any Surbiton
or Upper Norwood home.'*

exterior, and with imitation Tudor beams. Inside, the rooms had fumed oak fireplaces with white ornamental mirrors over them. There were stained glass fanlights and Lambeth Doulton tiles. 'Indistinguishable,' reported Nicholson, 'from those of any Surbiton or Upper Norwood home.'

It nevertheless suited the family and five of the six children were born there. Princess Mary thought it small but charming. Guests were often shocked at its confines and searched for places to store their luggage. One asked where the doctors at royal births managed to find room for their professional equipment.

Prince Edward in *A King's Story* provides the most intimate description of the house where he spent so much of his infancy. '. . . down the passage, with a swinging door in between, were two small, simply furnished rooms set apart for the children. In these two rooms my conscious memories began. One was called the Day Nursery. There we had our meals; there I learned to walk and was taught the alphabet and how to count. The other and larger of the two rooms was called the Night Nursery. In the late 1890s, when there were three of us children, Bertie, Mary and myself, we all slept in this one room with a nurse.

'There we were bathed in round tin tubs filled from cans of hot water brought upstairs by servants from a distant part of the house. Our windows looked out over the pond, and the quacking of the wild duck that lived there supplied a pleasant pastoral note at dawn and dusk. Across the pond, was the park where small, web–antlered Japanese deer roamed and grazed peacefully.'

Given the sunny nature of Edward and the compliance of his younger brother Albert, it is astonishing that one of their nurses carried out a campaign of tyranny against them lasting over three years. What is perhaps more astonishing is that the cruelty went undetected. Whether it was jealousy, or possessiveness – the woman wanting to keep the royal child to herself – is difficult to establish. The facts were recorded by Edward himself, however, for he remembered the bruises too well. Each afternoon when the time came for him to visit his parents in the drawing room she would pause outside the door and give the child a vicious pinch on the arm, an affront strong enough to set the toddler howling. It seemed to Prince George and Princess Mary that every time they saw this boy he was weeping and, neither being of a patient nature, he was quickly kissed and bundled away. This treatment went on for three years – and within the confines of a house as modest as York Cottage – before it was exposed and the woman dismissed. She was also blamed for forceably feeding the baby Albert from a bottle in a jolting carriage, giving him the beginnings of a lifelong suffering from indigestion.

One nurse had already been sent on her way for insolence to the

Albert with his mother Princess Mary. A shy child, later plagued with a stutter, he was overshadowed by his brothers and sister. In later life he overcame all handicaps.

Duchess of Teck, but now a third, the admirable Mrs Bill, arrived to take over in the nursery and she remained for many years. The children called her 'Lalla'.

Prince Edward was the most appealing of little boys and a great favourite of Queen Victoria. He alone was permitted to climb on the knee of the aged Queen and to kiss her on the cheek. Most royal children had to be satisfied, and probably were, with a pat of the old lady's hand. 'A delightful child,' was the elderly monarch's verdict. 'So intelligent, nice and friendly.' When he was beginning to walk and talk he called her "Gangan". One day at Balmoral he said to his great-grandmother, trying to pull her from her chair at lunch, 'Get up Gangan'. When she royally remained seated he caused great hilarity by calling an Indian servant and, pointing to the monarch, giving the instructions: 'Man – pull it.'

When the great Queen died the little boy inquired as to whether there were kings and queens in heaven and on being told it was unlikely he replied: 'Gangan won't like it.'

Edward's charm and informality even as a toddler endeared him to all. A visiting outfitter to York House hesitated to disturb the King, but the small prince, emerging from the nursery, said: 'There's nobody there that matters at all – only grandpa.' He recognized, at an early age, his responsibilities as the eldest son and often referred to his brothers and sister as 'the children'.

His younger brother, Albert, was much less forthcoming, more timid, and his father was ever ready to remind him of his duty in life. On his fifth birthday he was reminded: 'Now that you are five years old, I hope you will try and be obedient and do at once what you are told, as you will find it will come much easier to you the sooner you begin.'

All these strictures were to have an effect on a small boy who had been cruelly bullied by a nurse; was shy to the point of being timid; who needed to struggle in the schoolroom, and who was overshadowed by the outgoing personality of his older brother. Worse, it was decided that he had knock-knees and that he could be cured through splints on his legs. Thus through his early childhood he was required to wear these gruesome callipers during most of his waking hours and while he slept. When his elder brother went to naval college at Osborne, Albert was made 'Head boy' of the royal schoolroom, but was found to be disappointing by the tutor. He had a retiring demeanour and once, at some sort of children's function, he was told by his younger sister: 'Smile, and keep on smiling.' He did.

There were happy moments, most of them associated with his grandparents. Grandmama, Queen Alexandra, sometimes arrived to bathe the children whether or not it was bathtime, and was happy to make a great show of swallowing a drink which she knew the children had doctored with pepper and salt. Albert laughed with the rest. One day he attempted to interrupt his grandfather, the King, at a lunch and was told gently to keep quiet. He retired into his shell only to be asked afterwards what he had been trying to say. He pointed out that he had seen a caterpillar on the royal salad, but it was too late now because His Majesty had eaten it!

His stammer arrived at the age of seven, to increase his burdens, and was oddly blamed on the pronunciation of his German ancestors. He did, however, eventually become an accomplished sportsman. He was more than competent at football and cricket. At Dartmouth College today there is a mounted cricket ball with which he performed the hat-trick in a family match at Windsor, bowling out with successive deliveries King Edward VII, his grandfather, The Prince of Wales, his father, and Prince Edward, his brother; a feat unlikely to be equalled. He was also a splendid tennis player and in later years appeared in the men's doubles at Wimbledon. Eventually he conquered all and became a fine and much-loved monarch.

Princess Mary was more concerned, and more at ease, with her offspring when her husband was away. Under her remote exterior she loved them dearly. She kept a Baby Book in which the first step taken, the first words spoken and the first tooth appearing, were all recorded and which contained a lock of each child's hair. In her more maternal moments she taught them embroidery and Edward particularly became adept, enjoying the relaxation of the art throughout his life. During long journeys, or illness, he would while away the time by doing crochet work or making woollen garments for charity.

If Princess Mary was, and is, thought by some to have been a remote mother, her elder son was able to provide some warm and appealing moments from his memories. She would sing 'Swanee River' and 'The Camptown Races' with her little ones grouped around the piano. Once the cruelty of the 'pinching' nurse was no more, there were moments to savour. In *A King's Story* he recalled touchingly: 'It was my mother's habit to rest in her boudoir before dinner, and this hour she saved for us . . . She would be in a negligee resting on the sofa; and, when we were gathered around her on little chairs, she would read and talk to us . . . Her soft voice, her cultivated mind, the cosy room overflowing with personal treasures were all inseparable ingredients of the happiness associated with this last hour of a child's day.'

On 25 April 1897 their only daughter Victoria Alexandra Alice Mary was born. It was the year of Queen Victoria's Diamond Jubilee and a suggestion by her grandfather, Edward, Prince of Wales, that she should be named 'Diamond' was quickly put aside. She was a lively baby who grew into a tomboy, an energetic young lady and a fine horsewoman. As soon as she could walk she took to wandering about the farm buildings at Sandringham and was often to be seen sitting on a stool during milking time in the dairy. She shared the family aptitude for practical jokes and was said to be the ringleader of a plot against her brothers' French tutor, a Monsieur Hua, who told the children how much he enjoyed frogs' legs. Determined to get him some they only managed to fish tadpoles from the pond at Frogmore. These they persuaded the kitchen staff to cook and they were put before the unknowing Frenchman at lunch – on toast.

Mary's squeal of delight as the tutor took a first, anticipatory, bite into the poached tadpoles was the signal for helpless hilarity around the table. Monsieur Hua left, holding his handkerchief to his mouth, and Edward, as the senior child, was sent to apologize with as straight a face as he could muster.

The children spent hours 'fishing' in the pond with string and bent pins or paddling the flat-bottomed boat to its small island. For them, however, the great delight was the proximity of the 'Big House' where their indulgent grandparents were always happy to let them run riot, a welcome change from the restrictions, both parental and constructional, imposed by York Cottage.

Two months after the death of Queen Victoria in 1901 their parents left the country for an extended State Tour of Australia and the Empire, which was to last for eight months. The only-too-willing grandparents were left in charge of the exuberant youngsters. The enjoyment of these times was mutual; rules went out of the window and lessons were often ignored. '. . . they encouraged our innate boisterousness . . .' wrote Edward. '. . . I had passed temporarily under the sunny auspices of a grandfather who believed that lessons were less important to children than their happiness.'

Madame Helene Bricka, the ageing governess, was powerless to enforce the learning she was required to impart. After lunch with the children their grandfather, now, King Edward VII, would wave a smoke trail with his cigar and Alexandra smile encouragingly and tell the inquiring lady that it would not harm the children to be away from the schoolroom a little longer. The primers and pens could wait.

When the parents returned from their long trip to Australia they were shocked at the behaviour of the children and immediately called the governess and nanny to account. They explained, as respectfully as possible, that it was not their fault. After that a stronger hand, a footman, Frederick Finch was put in charge of the boys, as a sort of Nurse-Cum-Valet, and a few months later a tutor was engaged to formalise their schooling.

The children's year, like that of their parents, moved in an acknowledged orbit. Seasons were spent at Sandringham, at

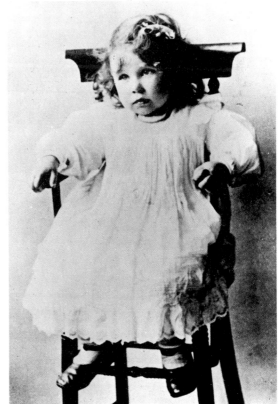

The little girl who became a beloved Queen Consort. Elizabeth Bowes-Lyon — the present Queen Mother — in childhood. Her early days were spent in Hertfordshire, and in the haunted castle of Glamis, Scotland.

*Elizabeth, youngest
daughter of the Earl and
Countess of Strathmore
with members of her family
in the drawing room of
Glamis Castle. It was at
Glamis that the young
Duke of York met and fell
in love with her.*

OPPOSITE: *George, born in 1902, became Duke of Kent and was killed while serving in the RAF in 1942.* ABOVE: *Princess Mary the only girl of the family, with her brothers Edward and Albert.* RIGHT: *Henry, born in 1900 at the height of the Boer War.*

A charming painting by Morgan and Blinks of Queen Alexandra, the ever-indulgent grandmother, with her three eldest grandchildren, Edward, Albert and Mary.

Marlborough House or York House in London, in Scotland, or at Frogmore, the house in Windsor Great Park that was given to George and Mary when they became Prince and Princess of Wales. Once the home of Queen Charlotte, it had a delightful walled garden but lacked electricity and proper heating.

Christmas at Sandringham was a delight for the children. They would be taken by their mother and father to the traditional gathering of the estate workers in the stable yard. Three hundred people, the men and their families, would gather there, the royal toddlers gazing with awe at the fresh-faced country children who gazed back with reciprocal wonder. Then there came a ritual which never failed to fascinate them – the inspection of the joints of beef, laid out or hung, each with its name label, and each dripping blood. The King would distribute the joints to the estate workers, and then the royal children would be taken back to York Cottage to change their clothes before going to the big house for their own gifts.

At Sandringham House everyone would gather in the ballroom and then Santa Claus would appear from the steward's room. No ceremonial state occasion could, for the children, equal that moment. There were huge Christmas trees – first popularized in Britain by the Prince Consort – holly, ivy and mistletoe. Presents were arranged on small tables, the children's gifts kept at a distance from those of the adults. It was a rule that toys were distributed last.

It would never have done for one of the expensive jewelled gifts which Edward gave to Alexandra (she had a collection of exquisite Fabergé animals) to have become the target for a bow and arrow or a popgun, and the habitual silver gifts from the Tsar had also to be cosseted. Even the household staff received their presents before the children, thus keeping the young ones on tenterhooks for as long as possible.

Their excitement was not always reserved for the unwrapping of their own presents. On at least one occasion the small princes had been smuggled into the room with instructions to change the labels on the servants' gifts, and the hilarity at seeing a footman confronted with a pair of ladies' stockings, was difficult to bottle up.

After the gifts the carol singers from the village came into the room and they sang as the Christmas darkness moved over the great open park.

A third son, Henry William Frederick Albert, was born at the height of the Boer War on 31 March 1900. Three of his mother's brothers were fighting in South Africa and, as royal recognition of the efforts of the army, Lord Roberts, the Commander-in-Chief, was selected as a godparent. He telegraphed his grateful acceptance from Bloemfontein. When the other children were shown the baby for the first time they

John, the youngest child of the family, who died aged thirteen.

inquired as to how it had arrived. Their mother told them that he had flown through the window. How did she know he would not fly out again? Ah, it had been necessary gently to clip his wings.

The new prince, who grew to become Duke of Gloucester, had the distinction of being the first son of a future king to be educated at school, as distinct from lessons at home with a succession of tutors. Not a strong boy he was sent to Broadstairs where he lodged at the home of his father's doctor. He was looked after by a nurse called Sister Edith and attended the local preparatory school, later going on to Eton.

His footsteps were followed by his next brother, George Edward Alexander Edmund, who was born at York Cottage on 20 December 1902. He became Duke of Kent in 1934 and was a great favourite with the British people. There was much grief when he was killed in an air crash while serving with the Royal Air Force in 1942.

The final child, John Charles Francis, was born in 1905. A gentle, tragic boy who suffered from epilepsy, he spent much of his childhood in a house apart, Wood Farm at Sandringham. His seizures so upset the other children – who loved him deeply – that it was decided he should live separately. He was looked after by the faithful Lalla at the farm and his grandmother Alexandra spent many hours with him because she feared he was lonely. He died in his sleep, at the age of thirteen, on 18 January 1919, and is buried in Sandringham churchyard beside the other Prince John, the child of Alexandra, who wrote to Mary, by now Queen: 'Now our two darling Johnnies lie side by side.' They were to be joined in that quiet churchyard by a baby of the same name, John Spencer, who died soon after birth in 1960. He would have been the elder brother of Princess Diana.

Chapter Four

The Children of King George VI

IF THERE EVER WAS A ROYAL BABY TO GIVE SHEER DELIGHT TO THE BRITISH people, a different emotion from the loyal interest in the infants of previous years, it was Princess Elizabeth Alexandra Mary – the present Queen.

To a country, indeed to a world, dragging itself from the horrors of the First World War, into the greyness and despondency brought by the Great Depression, this golden child, born on 21 April 1926, was a singular source of happiness and optimism. She was the only baby girl in the royal family at that time. Everybody loved her. It was said, without too much exaggeration, that the buses travelling down Piccadilly, past her parent's home at Number 145, tipped sideways so great was the movement of passengers on the upper deck hoping to catch a glimpse of her through the nursery window. Her nurse, Clara Knight, had to abandon secret walks with the pram in Hyde Park because the crowds became so huge that the police had trouble with the traffic, not to mention the safety of the Princess herself. Instead the baby had to be wheeled about the enclosed gardens of Buckingham Palace.

It would not be too much to say that her mother had brought a new quality of gentleness into the royal family. She had not expected, even when she married Prince Albert, Duke of York, to become Queen since Edward, Prince of Wales, was first in line to the throne. However, her humanity and good sense were a wonderful addition to a family still beset by the stringencies of the Victorian days.

From childhood Albert had been under the shadow of his elder brother. He was shy, gentle and plagued with a stutter. He could not pronounce the letters K–G–Q– and N, so that saying 'King and Queen' proved beyond him and he always referred to 'Their Majesties'. And yet his marriage to Elizabeth Bowes-Lyon resulted in a monarchy that was held in the hearts of the British people, and continues to be remembered as such. King George (as he became) and Queen Elizabeth refused to leave London during the most deadly days and nights of the German bombing, and Londoners have never forgotten. Their presence, as much as that of Churchill himself, helped to give heart and courage to a city, and a nation.

Elizabeth Angela Marguerite Bowes-Lyon, born on 4 August 1900, was the second youngest of the ten children of Lord and Lady Glamis. This old and aristocratic Scottish family lived, curiously, in homely Hertfordshire, in an exquisitely-gardened house called St Paul's at Walden Bury, near Hitchin. At four years of age she became Lady Elizabeth Bowes-Lyon when her father succeeded to the titles of the 14th Earl of Strathmore.

She first met Prince Albert, her future husband, at a children's party given by Lady Leicester in London, but it was not until many years had gone by that they were to meet again. Albert was visiting Glamis Castle, as a guest of the Earl and Countess of Strathmore. The Countess was ill and the twenty-one-year old Elizabeth became his hostess. He, a shy and uncertain young man, plagued by his speech impediment, with memories of a stern father and his 'terrifying' great-grandmother Victoria, not to mention the sadism of a nurse, had never been comfortable in society. Here he found himself in the company of a wise, gentle and beautiful young woman. When they married on 26 April 1923, in Westminster Abbey it was the first time for more than 650 years that the son of a reigning sovereign had been wed beneath that ancient roof – since 1269 when Edmund Crouchback, Earl of Lancaster and son of Henry III, was married there. The marriage of Albert and Elizabeth was also the first occasion in two and a half centuries that a prince in direct succession to the throne had married a commoner with royal consent.

For a while the couple lived at White Lodge, Richmond, Queen Mary's old home, but it proved too far from London for the many engagements that the young couple were expected to undertake. For three years they lived in rented or borrowed homes when they were in London until they finally found a home of their own, 145 Piccadilly.

Princess Elizabeth Alexandra Mary was born on 21 April 1926 at two-forty in the morning at 17, Bruton Street, the home of her maternal grandparents. Prince Albert's lily font, which had done service for so many years, was brought from Windsor for the christening in the chapel at Buckingham Palace at six-thirty in the evening. Water brought from the River Jordan was sprinkled on the baby's forehead and she was then taken away to her bed by her nurse, Clara Knight, (her mother's old nurse), while the grown-ups sat down to a sumptuous dinner in her honour.

When she was eight months old her parents, as Duke and Duchess of York, were required to leave for a visit to Australia and New Zealand

OPPOSITE: *The Duchess of York with her first-born child, Elizabeth, born in April 1926.* ABOVE: *The Duke and Duchess of York with Princess Elizabeth. Shortly after this photograph was taken the young couple left for an overseas tour which lasted for six months. The baby remained with her grandparents.*

from which they did not return for a further six months. The parting was very sad, felt not only by the parents but by every mother in the country. Elizabeth was given, as a parting present, a string of coral beads, which she often wore. Her mother, recalling the departure, remembered how the little girl had held onto the brass buttons of her father's naval uniform. 'It quite broke me up,' recalled the Duchess. 'It was as if she did not want him to go.'

Until she was fourteen months old Elizabeth shared her days with both sets of grandparents, at the pretty country house at Walden Bury and the huge space of Buckingham Palace. When her parents returned the crowds in London were so great that they had to carry the golden-haired girl to the balcony of their new house overlooking Piccadilly to show her to the people. The cheering and excitement were enormous. The Princess waved and the great throng responded. The Duke noted with modest good humour: 'My chief claim to fame seems to be that I am the father of Princess Elizabeth.'

Her parents had, of course, come back laden with presents for the toddler. Apart from tropical birds and other livestock, there was a set of doll's house furniture from Tasmania, a teddy bear 'for Princess Betty' from Brisbane, larger-than-life sized dolls from New Zealand, and two threepenny pieces from two children in Adelaide 'for her moneybox'. Two outback Aboriginals subscribed ten shillings for the same cause, but were ushered away as they were about to make the gift. 'I think the only mistake I made in the tour,' said the Duchess, 'was not to make sure I accepted the ten shillings.'

King George V, in contrast to his stern upbringing of his own children, doted on the little girl. She called him 'Grandpapa England' and he willingly joined in her nursery games, including one where he became a horse and, on all fours, was led around the room by his beard.

When the parents were abroad the King wrote to them: 'Your sweet little daughter is growing daily. She has four teeth now, which is quite good at eleven months old. She is very happy.'

On the royal couple's return from their tour, when the princess had returned to her parent's home, the King discovered that from a certain window in Buckingham Palace he could, with the aid of binoculars, see the nursery window at 145 Piccadilly, and he would wait, watching, until Elizabeth waved.

When the King became ill and eventually went to Bognor Regis to recuperate Lilibet, as she was always called within the family, was taken down by her nurse to raise his spirits. They played at sandcastles which were so splendid that the visiting Archbishop of Canterbury was of the opinion that he had never seen better. They should, he suggested, be railed off and preserved.

George was not alone in his admiration for the happy, curly-haired

Princess Elizabeth, aged one, beloved by the British People. Her father good-humouredly said once:
'My chief claim to fame seems to be that I am the father of Princess Elizabeth.'

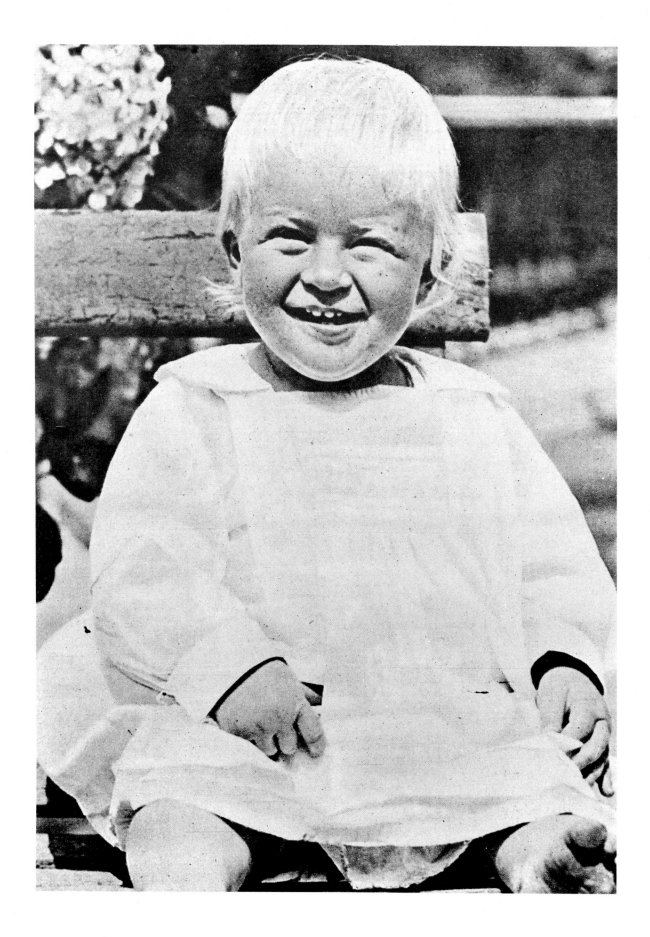

OPPOSITE: *A smiling Prince Philip, aged one, poses at the wedding of his uncle, Lord Mountbatten.* ABOVE: *Philip, aged three, with his mother in 1924.*

child. Even Winston Churchill, no admirer of infants, fell under her spell. On a visit to Balmoral he wrote to his wife Clementine: 'There is no one here at all except the family, the household and Princess Elizabeth, aged two. The latter is a character. She has an air of authority and reflectiveness astonishing in an infant.'

Others noticed the same endearing authority. One morning at Windsor, Sir Owen Morshead, watched the officer of the guard, an imposing figure, with sword, stride like a giant across to the perambulator in which sat the tiny Elizabeth. 'Permission to march off, please, Ma'am,' he requested in his most formidable military tone. The response was an inclination of the bonneted head and a wave of the woolly-gloved hand. She knew a salute when she saw it and always raised her hand in acknowledgement. At Glamis, on a visit to her mother's home, she looked around, puzzled, and inquired: 'Where are my sentries?'

Glamis Castle in Angus, one of the most romantic and evocative castles in Scotland, goes back a thousand years into history. It is said to have a secret room known only to each heir of the Earl of Strathmore, and it has associations with Macbeth. It was there on a suitably stormy night in 1930 that Princess Margaret Rose was born.

The Duchess of York, despite the imminent arrival of her baby, decided to go to Glamis as usual in August. Mr J R Clynes, the Home Secretary was despatched to authenticate the birth of the royal baby and dutifully made the long journey, but stayed at Airlie Castle nine miles away. In the event the weather was so foul on the night of the birth that he did not reach Glamis until the new child was wrapped and sleeping. It was the last time that the archaic custom of a government witness being present at the birth of a royal child was carried out. The next royal baby, Prince Charles in 1948, arrived without such authentication.

Mr Clynes, however, was enthusiastic enough after his thunder and lightning journey, to pronounce that he had never seen a finer baby. Like her elder sister Elizabeth, she was delivered by Caesarean section and weighed 6 lb 11 ounces.

There were bonfires lit that night in the village of Glamis for was this not the first princess to be born in Scotland for more than three hundred years? Pipes played and there was a raising of glasses.

The small village had a shop-cum-post-office and it was there that births were recorded by the registrar. The Duke of York eventually went to the little shop to fulfil this duty, but only after a careful delay. The Duchess had noticed beforehand that the next entry in the register was numbered 13, so the parents decided to wait until another child had been registered before recording the birth of their daughter.

They had chosen the names Ann Margaret, but for some reason King George V actively opposed the first name. He simply did not like it, he

ABOVE: *Early in life
Elizabeth learned some
royal requirements – such as
waving to the crowds.
Winston Churchill said:
'She has an air of authority
and reflectiveness
astonishing in an infant.'*
RIGHT: *Elizabeth, in 1929,
with her nanny, Clara
Knight, on her way to
Sandringham for
Christmas.*

said. So, on 30 October, in the private chapel at Buckingham Palace, the child was christened Margaret and Rose after one of the sisters of the Duchess.

The house at 145 Piccadilly, was next door but one to Apsley House, once the Duke of Wellington's home. There was a fine glass dome at the top of the building (through which a bomb fell during the war). On the landing were stabled Princess Elizabeth's collection of more than thirty toy horses. Not for her the preoccupation with dolls that had been the fascination of little girls in the royal family since Victoria's time. Elizabeth's horses were fed, watered, saddled and bridled every day by the toddler who soon acquired, however, an interest in the real animal which has never left her.

She and Margaret Rose could look from the nursery window onto the traffic in Piccadilly. There were still many horse-drawn vehicles in London at that time and they loved to watch the delivery carts, particularly those drawn by the great dray horses, as they vied with the motor vehicles in the street. Faces pressed to the pane they would shout encouragement to any horse and driver engaged in a traffic battle with the noisy motor cars and vans.

The night nursery contained two white beds, decorated with pink roses. Each princess had her own set of china. Elizabeth's was decorated with a design of a pair of magpies and the words 'Two for Joy' and Margaret's with lovebirds and heather. The toys in the nursery included a wooden chair from Switzerland, carved with chamois which, disconcertingly, played a voluntary by an alpenhorn when anyone sat on it. It was to this chair that occasional visitors were shown.

Always a dedicated and serious child, Elizabeth was not, however, beyond showing rebellion in the schoolroom, which was a small annex to the drawing room. On one occasion, miffed at some instruction from a tutor, she quietly placed the inkwell on her head and let the contents run over her forehead and down her face. She was deeply interested in royalty. She kept a photo album and scrapbook about royal children, going far back into the distant reaches of European royalty, especially those descended through Queen Victoria. Any pieces of information which she read on the subject she entered in the book, and she would receive photographs from various relatives and visitors to the house who knew of her interest. One of the fascinations was tracing how she herself was descended and related to the people in her scrapbook.

To go to Glamis was always a treat for the princesses. They would ride a docile pony to the little Scottish station to watch the trains go by and, when their mount grew restive, he was accommodated in the waiting room.

Marion Crawford – 'Crawfie' to the children – who was their governess, revealed many of these intimate childhood moments in her

TIME

The Weekly Newsmagazine

"P'INCESS LILYBET"

She has set the babe fashion for yellow.

(See FOREIGN NEWS)

Volume XIII

Number 17

Royal Cover Girl. To the Americans, the young princess was like a film star.

A princess at play. There was tremendous public interest in the young daughter of the Duke and Duchess of York, so much so that her nanny had to stop taking her for walks in public because of the pressure of the crowds.

book *The Little Princesses*, for which she was roundly criticized. It does, however, give some insight into the daily lives of the children which was devoured by a public which adored them. Read today, when royal servants are forbidden to reveal their lives in service, it is hardly sensational and contains some intriguing anecdotes. She tells of J M Barrie going to Glamis as a guest and finding himself opposite the infant Princess Margaret. Between them was a tempting cracker and Barrie asked the little girl whether it was hers or his. 'It is yours and mine,' replied the princess. Barrie put the line 'It's yours and mine' into his play *The Boy David*, promising a royalty of one penny every time the line was spoken on the stage. He kept his word and after his death Lady Cynthia Asquith, who for many years had been his secretary, appeared at Buckingham Palace with a bagful of pennies.

Royal children, used to large rooms and unending corridors, were always the happy recipients of small houses in which they could play at being ordinary people. Victoria's children had enjoyed the intimacy of the Swiss cottage at Osborne House and Elizabeth and Margaret Rose were just as entranced with the gift of a miniature Welsh cottage from the people of the Principality. It was called *Y Bwthyn Bach To Gwelt* – The Little Cottage with the Straw Roof. The straw roof caused trouble for, during its journey on the back of a lorry from Cardiff, this roof caught fire, much to the consternation of the unfortunate driver. The charred little house was taken back to Cardiff for repairs and was eventually delivered safely to Princess Elizabeth, late for her birthday.

Both girls enjoyed the closeness of the cottage, two-fifths normal size, measuring twenty-two feet by eight feet by fifteen feet high. It was complete in every detail, tiny tables, chairs and bookcase, a gas cooker and a refrigerator in the kitchen, crockery on the Welsh dresser and in the drawers cutlery – and a tiny insurance policy, which had apparently not been of much use when the roof caught fire! Over the mantlepiece was a miniature reproduction of a portrait of the children's mother, the Duchess of York, painted by the Welsh artist Sybil Charlotte Williams.

The delight of the children on seeing the chintz curtains and the small bed was only exceeded by the bathroom, which contained a three foot four inch long bath with hot and cold running water. The Welsh cottage was erected in the rose garden at Royal Lodge, Windsor, which the Duke and Duchess used as their country home. Royal Lodge had been given to the young couple by King George in 1931. It was originally designed by Nash the famous architect for the Prince Regent, although by this time it was in a somewhat dilapidated state and surrounded by deeply overgrown gardens. The family enjoyed putting it to rights. The Duchess, particularly, loved the reclaiming of the garden from the dandelions and bindweed for she had inherited her mother's skill and enthusiasm as a horticulturist.

A future Queen at five. George V said he prayed that nothing would come between Elizabeth and the Throne.

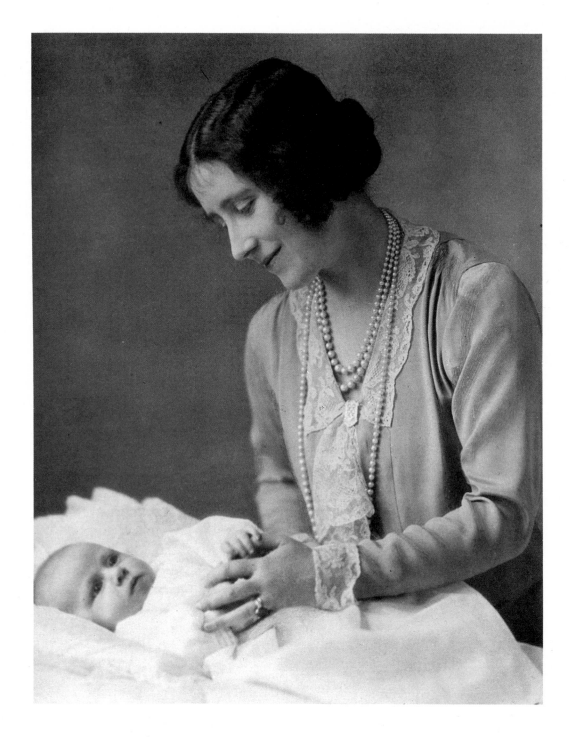

Princess Margaret Rose with the Duchess of York. Born on a stormy August night in 1930 at Glamis Castle, Margaret was the first princess born in Scotland for over 300 years.

Margaret, aged one, with her mother. The registration of her birth was delayed to avoid the number 13 in the Glamis register.

*At the door of St Paul's.
The royal family enter the
cathedral for a
Thanksgiving Service to
mark the Silver Jubilee of
King George V and Queen
Mary in 1935. The King
and Queen lead the way,
Princesses Elizabeth and
Margaret are behind the
Prince of Wales, later the
Duke of Windsor. Their
mother is glancing towards
them.*

ABOVE LEFT: *Margaret Rose, aged two, with her sister in the nursery at Walden Bury, their mother's home.*
LEFT & OPPOSITE: *Margaret Rose was a charmer with an overflowing sense of humour, who was indulged by everyone. Her father said she was the sort of child who could persuade a pearl out of an oyster.*

Public attention was concentrated on Elizabeth, with Margaret Rose often in the background and this gave rise to an extraordinary rumour that she was deaf and dumb. She remained, however, a frequently solitary child and, as with many children, sometimes played with an invisible companion who, in this case, was imaginatively called 'Cousin Halifax'.

The two small princesses were different characters. Elizabeth dedicated and serious, as if already subconsciously aware of the life of duty that lay before her; Margaret, a charmer who was indulged by her parents and everyone who knew her. She was an accomplished mimic and had an overflowing sense of humour. 'Margaret,' said her father, 'is the sort of child who could persuade a pearl to come out of an oyster.'

They were, despite the differences, a fond and united family. The Duke and Duchess held no great respect for social life and, since they never expected to be called to the centre of the stage, were able to lead a quieter existence than that which was later to be thrust upon them. Each morning the two princesses would go into their parents' bedroom until it was time for breakfast and lessons. They would rejoin them after lunch and at bathtime in the evening the Duke and Duchess were always there among the bubbles and the steam. They tucked the children into bed and there were stories to be told.

This domesticity was accompanied by the family dogs, Mimsy, Stiffy and Scrummy, the golden labradors and the Welsh corgis Dookie and Jane. There were frequent visitors for 145 Picadilly was recognized as a family haven away from the social life of London. The Prince of Wales, the children's uncle, would call in for a game of cards with his nieces.

George V, the loving grandfather, gave Elizabeth her first pony named Peggy, and she delighted in riding it in Windsor Great Park under the scrutiny of the redoubtable Mr Owen, the groom, who was like God in the eyes of the little princess. He was her friend, confidant and adviser. Once her father, when asked his advice on some future matter, replied a little wryly: 'Don't ask me, ask Mr Owen. Who am I to make suggestions?'

Elizabeth, as she grew, continued to be loved for her gentleness and quietly happy nature. In 1935, shortly before he died, her grandfather George V said to Queen Mary, and was overheard by the Archbishop of Canterbury: 'I pray to God that my eldest son will never marry and have children and that nothing will come between Bertie, Lilibet and the throne.'

It was a moment of prophecy.

Chapter Five

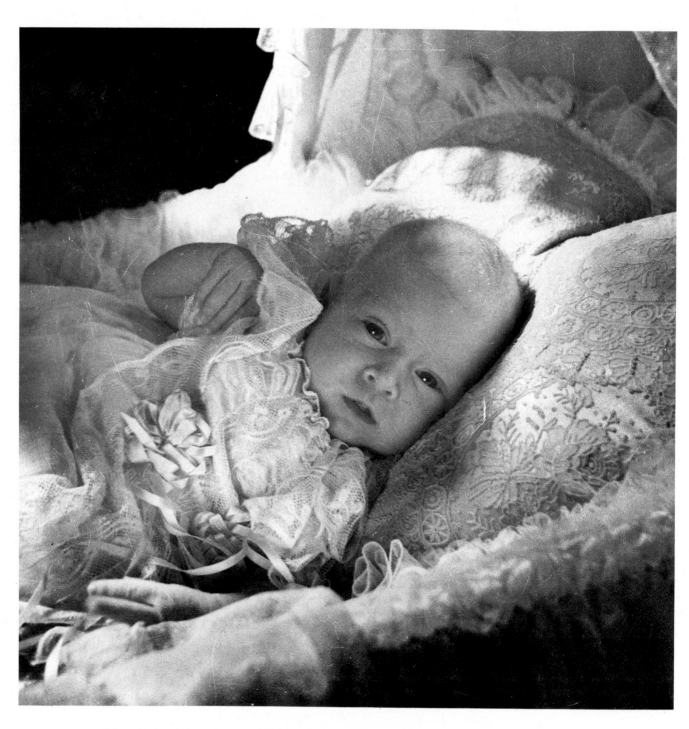

Prince Charles Philip Arthur George born at Buckingham Palace on 14 November 1948. It was the first time that the Home Secretary had not been called upon to authenicate a royal birth.

The Children of Queen Elizabeth II

IT WAS IN JULY 1939 THAT AN EIGHTEEN-YEAR-OLD SEA CADET AT Dartmouth Royal Naval College first met a girl of thirteen who was eventually to become his wife. The royal family had sailed into Dartmouth aboard the yacht *Victoria and Albert*, but because of an outbreak of mumps and chickenpox at the Royal Naval College it was considered prudent that Princess Elizabeth and her younger sister should not attend the Sunday morning service in the chapel. Instead they were sent to the home of Admiral Sir Frederick Dalrymple-Hamilton to play with his children. Here they met the young sea cadet Philip who, finding that playing with a model railway was somewhat boring, took the two princesses to the tennis court where he proceeded to try and impress them by jumping the net. Later he showed them around the grounds of the naval college.

On the following day the royal yacht sailed from the River Dart with a motley armada of small boats, manned by cadets, as an unofficial escort. As the vessel went out into the English Channel the little craft, one by one, dropped away until there was only one boat remaining, rowed furiously by a young man – Philip. Princess Elizabeth watched the brash but heroic figure through binoculars, and it took orders from the King, through a megaphone, before the youth turned back to the shelter of the estuary.

Years later, in his biography of King George VI, Sir John Wheeler-Bennett, describing the marriage of Princess Elizabeth and Philip, wrote: 'This was the man with whom Princess Elizabeth had been in love from their first meeting.'

That meeting took place only weeks before Europe was overcome by war, and during the years of hostilities Philip, a serving naval officer, saw Elizabeth only during home leaves. By the end of 1943 the relationship had deepened and in 1944 there were discussions with the King about a formal engagement. At that time, however, King George

ABOVE: *Charles at nineteen weeks and weighing sixteen pounds two ounces. His birth ensured the succession of the House of Windsor.* OPPOSITE: *Prince Charles aged one. Princess Elizabeth was twenty-two years when she had her first child.*

Prince Charles, aged two, enjoying a walk with Nanny Mabel Anderson.

was reluctant to give his consent. The war was still being heavily fought and the King considered that his daughter had led far too restricted and sheltered a life to consider marriage. It was not until war had been over for two years, on the 10 July 1947, that the final assent to a betrothal was given.

Prince Philip was the only son of Prince Andrew of Greece and Princess Alice of Battenberg, the great-granddaughter of Queen Victoria. He was born on 10 June 1921 on the Greek island of Corfu.

His family left Greece after an extraordinary episode of gunboat diplomacy instigated by King George V. News had been received in London that Philip's father, Prince Andrew, was imprisoned in Athens, a strong candidate for execution, following the upheaval caused by the defeat of the Greek armies by the Turkish forces of Mustapha Kemal Atatürk in 1922. The British monarch, so recently distressed by the fate of the Russian royal family at the hands of revolutionaries, immediately ordered the dispatch of a light cruiser, *HMS Calypso*, to rescue the family. Under the guns of the British Royal Navy the family was brought to the cruiser which weighed anchor without delay and set sail. Philip was a year old. He was accommodated in a makeshift cot made from orange boxes.

Thereafter, Philip's parents lived fragmented lives. His father although haunted by financial problems still did the rounds of the European season, spending much time in Monte Carlo and on the French Riviera. His mother settled in a small house in the St Cloud area of Paris where Philip attended a school for expatriates. Although his parents were of modest means they had many royal relatives and friends. His cousin, who became Queen Alexandra of Yugoslavia, recalls a childhood where holidays were spent circulating around a network of European relations where even the children's nannies would tuck into bowls of caviar at tea-time.

In 1930 his mother and father separated. Philip was brought first to stay with his grandmother, the Marchioness of Milford Haven, at Kensington Palace while his Uncle George, who was his guardian, arranged for him to enter Cheam Preparatory School in Surrey.

His mother returned to Greece where she remained throughout the German occupation during the Second World War. She founded the Christian Sisterhood of Martha and Mary and was seen throughout the rest of her life in the grey habit of the order.

In 1933 Philip left Cheam School and, in what must have been a sharp contrast, joined Salem School, by Lake Constance in Bavaria, run by the stern educationalist Kurt Hahn. Eventually Hahn removed his establishment to Gordonstoun, a house in Morayshire.

A musical prince. LEFT:
*Charles unofficially
conducts the massed bands
at the Trooping of the
Colour ceremony in 1950.*
ABOVE: *He attempts a
few notes on a toy
trumpet. He was a placid,
good-humoured and
thoughtful child.* OPPOSITE:
*Charles appears to be
giving much thought to
getting into a toy car.*

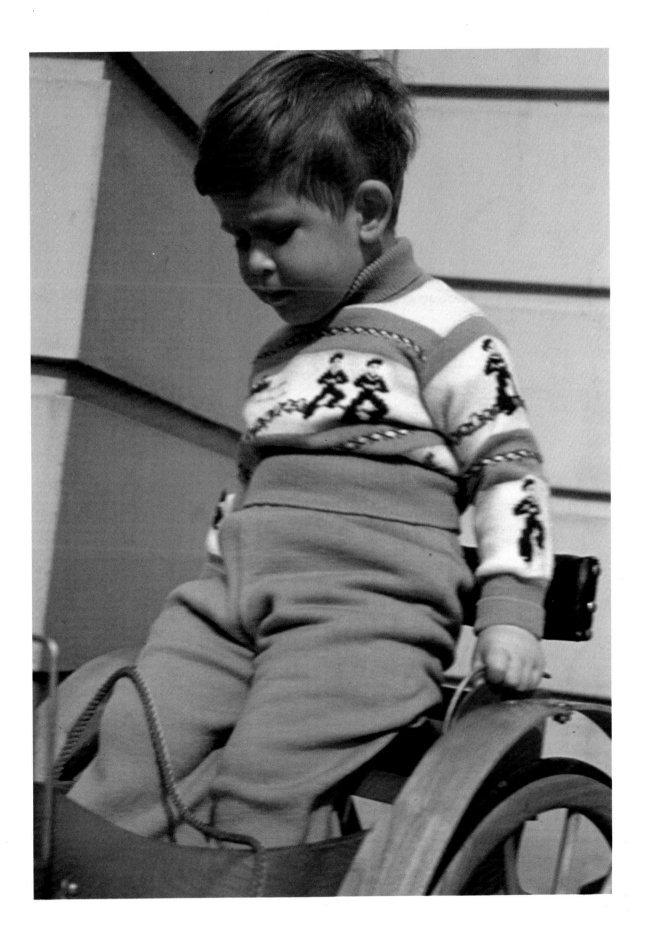

To say that a royal wedding was just the thing the weary nation needed in 1947 is an understatement. In Britain rationing was still in force, and the winter had been the most severe for many years. That summer the young couple were feted wherever they went. They had given the nation something to smile about.

They were married in Westminster Abbey on the 20 November, 1947, Philip being created Duke of Edinburgh on the previous day. After their honeymoon Philip had to return to his naval duties.

Just under a year later Princess Elizabeth gave birth to her first child, Prince Charles. She had been living the life of a naval wife in Malta, where her husband was a lieutenant on *HMS Chequers*. He returned to London in ample time for the birth, but Philip's final timing was awry – when the baby was born at 9.14 pm on 14 November 1948, he was playing squash with his private secretary. The game was left unfinished.

Crowds had gathered in front of the Buckingham Palace railings in expectation of an announcement. The radio news had said that the midwife was staying the night. Then a page emerged from the great, grey building and whispered to a police inspector, who, cupping his hands, turned to the crowd and shouted: 'It's a Prince!'

The crowd remained in front of the palace for hours, singing and cheering, pushing forward to read the official bulletin pinned on the notice board, until an official appeared and told them that the Princess appreciated the singing but it was preventing her from sleeping. The throng quietly dispersed.

Charles Philip Arthur George was the first royal child to be born without the presence of the Home Secretary being required. The King had personally seen to it that this anachronism was removed, thus saving the cabinet minister both a journey and an embarrassment.

In those days the grim hand of austerity was still on the land. A cot was brought from a storeroom, a miniature hundred-year-old four poster, which had last been used by the baby Duke of Kent in 1902. The perambulator used by both his mother and his aunt, Princess Margaret, was also brought out, dusted, refurbished and pressed into use. It was a huge, ungainly vehicle, and Nurse Helen Lightbody could be seen trundling it like an artillery piece under the wintry trees of St James's Park. Prince Charles' first toy was an ivory-handled rattle which his mother had sounded from her baby carriage. It was a sign of the times that to celebrate the birth of her child the princess sent food parcels to the mothers of all babies born on the same day.

The old schoolroom at Buckingham Palace was turned into a nursery with Mrs Lightbody and Nurse Mabel Anderson, both firm kind Scots ladies, as the staff. Nurse Lightbody was not married, the 'Mrs' being a courtesy title as she was the senior nurse.

The Chapel at the Palace had been bombed during the Blitz on

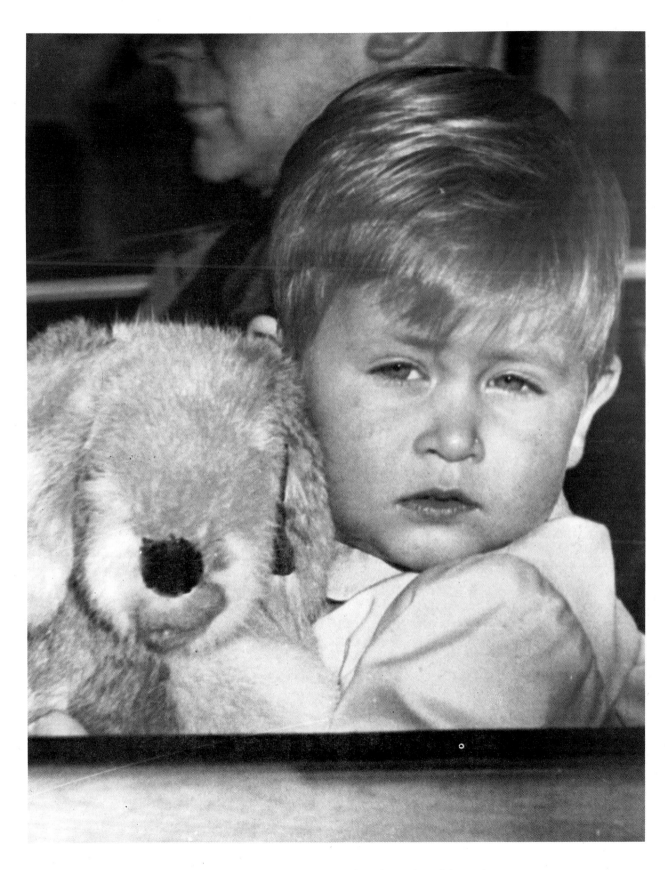

Charles, and companion, look from the window of the royal car.

Princess Elizabeth and the Duke of Edinburgh with two-year-old Prince Charles and baby Princess Anne, photographed at their then home, Clarence House, in 1950.

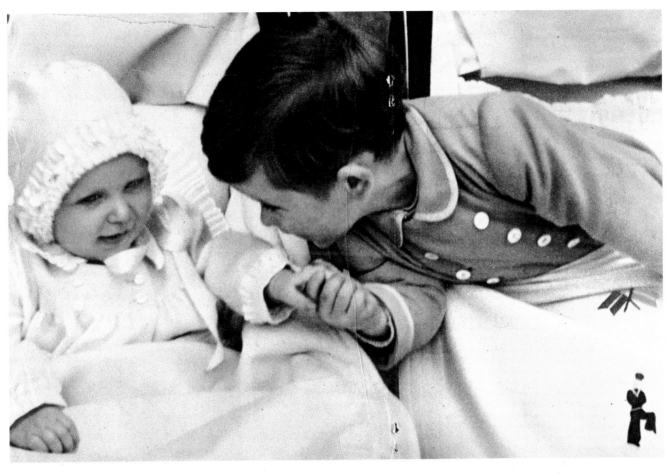

ABOVE: *Prince Charles confides a secret to his sister Anne.* RIGHT: *Prince Charles and Princess Anne pose for a photograph with their mother while on holiday at Balmoral in 1952.*

A lively and inquisitive Anne amuses her parents. These photographs were taken shortly before the couple left for a tour of Canada and the USA in 1951. ABOVE: *A royal corgi guards Charles and Anne in this photograph taken in 1951.* RIGHT: *The children, dressed alike, at Balmoral in the following year.*

Princess Anne, standing between her mother and her Aunt Margaret, shows great interest in a brooch. Princess Margaret later became the mother of two children, Viscount Linley and Lady Sarah Armstrong-Jones.
OPPOSITE: *Princess Anne, aged 2¾, in a charming portrait by Stella Marks.*

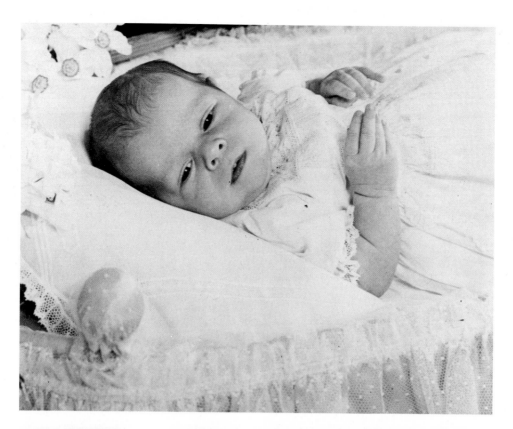

Prince Andrew was the first child born to a reigning monarch since Beatrice, Queen Victoria's youngest daughter, in 1857. ABOVE AND BELOW: *Prince Andrew at his christening in 1960 with his family.*

Holiday at Balmoral, 1960. After an interval of almost ten years since the birth of Princess Anne, the Queen found that she was able to spend more time with her third child, Andrew.

The Queen and Prince Andrew with corgis in attendance.

Andrew, as a toddler, shows the infectious grin which has become famous.

London and had not been restored, so the christening of the new prince was held in the Music Room. Dr Fisher, Archbishop of Canterbury, sprinkled water on the child's forehead. The godparents were King George VI, the Queen, King Haakon of Norway, the Hon. David Bowes-Lyon, Prince George of Greece, Princess Margaret, the Dowager Marchioness of Milford Haven (Prince Philip's grandmother) and Lady Brabourne, the daughter of Earl Mountbatten.

Queen Mary, the frail Queen Mother, gave to the baby a silver gilt cup once owned by George III. Touchingly she recorded in her diary: 'I gave a present from my great-grandfather to my great-grandson – 168 years later.'

Prince Philip was still a serving officer with the Mediterranean Fleet and Princess Elizabeth spent as much time as she could in Malta with her husband, the baby remaining in Mrs Lightbody's charge in the nursery at Clarence House. Two years later he was joined by a baby sister, Princess Anne, the first royal child to be born at Clarence House. When she was born on 15 August 1950 she weighed six pounds and had a mop of dark hair. Philip was on this occasion at a further distance than the squash court – in the Mediterranean – but this time he arrived in time for the birth.

When he went to register the birth of the girl – Anne Elizabeth Alice Louise – Philip was handed a ration book, an identity card and orange juice and cod liver oil. The war was over but there was still rationing, and the newly-formed Welfare State was much in evidence. Prince Charles was delighted with his sister and, when 'Nana' – Nurse Lightbody – was not around he would invite any visitor to Clarence House to 'Come and see the new baby'.

Princess Elizabeth was still moving between London and the naval quarters in Malta but, with the failing health of King George, she and the Duke of Edinburgh found themselves with more and more official engagements. Philip, enjoying his first command, as Lieutenant Commander of the frigate *HMS Magpie*, had to take indefinite leave in July 1951, and return with his wife to London.

It was decided that a planned tour of East Africa, Australia and New Zealand should be undertaken by the young couple and on 31 January 1952, they set out for Kenya. They were at the famous Tree Tops Hotel when the news came through that on 6 February King George VI had died in his sleep at Sandringham. Elizabeth, at twenty-five, was Queen of England. Her slight, lonely figure at the top of the aircraft steps as she arrived back in mourning London is not easily forgotten.

In the following year, Coronation Year, the elderly, ever-austere, Queen Mary, also died. The last link with the past was broken. People spoke of a new Elizabethan age.

The Coronation was televised and seen by millions of people, many

Prince Edward Anthony Richard Louis born in 1964, with the Queen and his brother, Andrew. The crib in which the baby lies was also used when the Queen and Princess Margaret were babies.

Andrew's confident pose for the photographer is not reflected in the studied expression of his baby brother, Edward. Both these photographs were taken by Cecil Beaton.

ABOVE: *Royal children at play in the sitting room at Windsor Castle. Edward amuses himself with a toy corgi. Andrew puts items — including silhouettes of jet fighters — into his scrapbook.* OPPOSITE: *The Queen waves to the crowds after the Trooping of the Colour, 1965. Edward seems less sure of his part.*

ABOVE: *Edward, aged two, in the grounds of Buckingham Palace follows the family interest in gardening. His grandmother and great-grandmother were expert gardeners.* OPPOSITE: *Autumnal activity in the palace grounds. The young Princes take up leaves but one of the corgis hinders operations.*

Edward among the fallen leaves beside the lake at Buckingham Palace.

watching television for the first time. It was the first big occasion Prince Charles attended. His baby sister had been outraged when she realised that she was to be left out. Princess Anne can still recall her indignation as Charles was borne off to Westminster Abbey in the royal limousine.

The toddler provided an eye-catching sideshow while the long and solemn ceremony was taking its course. He stood on a stool in the Royal Gallery between the Queen Mother and Princess Margaret, who managed, with patience but some difficulty, to keep him from tumbling over the rail or stealing the show in other ways. He pointed to the finery and to the people and asked his grandmother questions. After an hour his head disappeared from view altogether and people, watching from the corners of their eyes, wondered if he had been taken home by a nurse. But no, he appeared triumphantly again, now standing on a stool and clutching the handbag of 'Granny Royal', as he called the Queen Mother.

During his parents' prolonged absences, his grandmother devoted much of her time, and ingenuity, to amusing the small boy. (She had once seen a magic show and was so taken with one of the tricks that she asked the conjuror if he would teach her how to do it. He was delighted and, at the next family gathering, she proceeded to perform the illusion to the delight of Charles and the astonishment of the rest of the family. Charles then dubbed her 'Granny Royal – the Magician'.)

The young Queen and her Consort moved into Buckingham Palace in May 1952, and a nursery suite was prepared on the second floor (rather more conveniently placed than Queen Victoria's first nursery there). It had a nursery room, a sitting room for Nurse Lightbody, two bedrooms, a bathroom and a small kitchen. The furniture was bright and functional. There were two glass-fronted cabinets, a gift from Queen Mary, to store the children's special treasures. Anne prized her miniature tea service and two golden elephants with enamel trappings, given to her by Earl Mountbatten, her godfather, while Charles kept his picture books and toy motor cars there. His favourite toy was a large blue, increasingly battered teddy bear.

Queen Elizabeth always remembered how much the presence of her parents had meant to her as a small child. Now she and the Duke made a point of spending half an hour with their children every morning, and a further hour or so at night for games and stories and bathtime, notwithstanding all the pressing appointments of state.

The prince and the princess had contrasting personalities. Charles was thoughtful, sensitive and slow to annoy. Anne was more outgoing, noisy and occasionally given to stamping her foot. Charles had his naughty moments, however, and on one occasion was prevented by Nurse Lightbody from going on an outing to Windsor, where the chaplain's son was a popular playmate. Anne went instead, going off

Baby Diana Spencer on her first birthday at Park House.

Park House, Sandringham, leased in 1935 to Lord Fermoy, Diana's grandfather, by King George V.

with that special triumph which small sisters have when they know they have achieved some degree of one-upmanship over an elder brother.

Almost before she could walk Princess Anne was interested in horses. It was with scarcely concealed chagrin that some years later she saw her brother being given a present of a pony by the Russian leaders, Krushchev and Bulganin, during their visit to this country. She was presented with a bear. She gave the bear to the zoo.

Charles, too, was particularly fond of animals. He had an angora rabbit called Harvey; a Shetland pony, Cloudy, and a pair of lovebirds, Davy and Annie, after Davy Crockett and Annie (Get Your Gun) Oakley.

In November 1953 the Queen and the Duke went on a six-month tour of the world and the children had to be left behind. It was reminiscent of the moment years before when Elizabeth's own parents had been required to leave her behind for a long period. Charles and Anne were left in direct charge of Miss Peebles, who had become their governess, and the beloved 'Nana'. The parents were not due back until May but, as they drew nearer home, after all the miles and all the ceremonies, the Queen could not bear to be away from her children a moment longer.

Arrangements were made for the royal children, Miss Anderson, and Miss Peebles to board the *Royal Yacht Britannia* which was sailing out to Libya to meet the Queen and Prince Philip, and to transport them on the last stage of their long journey. The excitement of the two children was enormous as they made ready their tricycles and toys for the trip. On board four sailors were given the job of keeping an eye open for the safety of the two young passengers.

Elizabeth and Philip were standing on the balcony of the palace of King Idris in Tobruk when the white shape of the approaching yacht appeared over the blue horizon. It was a wonderful moment for the young parents.

After a gap of almost ten years Queen Elizabeth surprised the nation with the announcement that she was expecting another baby. Prince Andrew, called Andrew Albert Christian Edward, after his grandfathers and great-great-grandfathers, was born at the Palace on 19 February 1960. He was the first child to be born to a reigning monarch since Princess Beatrice was born to Queen Victoria in 1857. Mabel Anderson, who was now the royal nanny, was particularly delighted. Charles was at Cheam school and Anne was nine and a half years old. Now there was a real baby in the nursery.

The Queen found that she was able to devote much more time to this infant. When her previous children were young she had been an

Edward, aged two, looks out at a photographer looking in.

apprentice monarch, feeling her way, with only limited time to spend with them. Now she made time to be with the baby for a good portion of the day. On the nanny's day off, if it were at all possible, she looked after him, she taught him to count and helped him with his alphabet.

She also ensured, with her husband's agreement, that this child should, as far as was possible, be kept out of the limelight. No photographs were released to the press of the christening and Andrew was sixteen months old before he was seen officially in public.

Even after that he was rarely in the public eye, growing almost unnoticed into the extrovert youth, handsome, good at sports, who was fond of practical jokes. Who put bubble bath in the Windsor Castle swimming pool has never been fully discovered, although there have been grave suspicions; the same culprit, it was thought, who once tied together the bootlaces of a palace sentry.

Four years later Queen Elizabeth again surprised the country by the announcement that she was expecting a fourth child. On 10 March 1964, Prince Edward was born. He was christened on 2 May at Windsor Castle – Edward Anthony Richard Louis. Anthony was after his uncle Lord Snowdon, Princess Margaret's husband, Richard after Prince Richard of Gloucester, Louis after Prince Louis of Hesse. The godmothers were the Duchess of Kent and Princess George of Hanover.

Edward, a quiet, shy boy, was fortunate in his playmates. There were three other toddlers in the Buckingham Palace nursery; James, the first son of Princess Alexandra and Mr Angus Ogilvy; Sarah, the daughter of his aunt, Princess Margaret; and the Duchess of Kent's daughter, Helen. All four babies had been born in the same year.

As always, holidays were spent at Sandringham and they were there joined by another playmate, one of the daughters of their neighbours and old friends, Lord and Lady Althorp. She was a pretty, lively, fair-headed child, a year younger than Prince Andrew. Her name was Diana Frances and in 1981 she married the Prince's elder brother Charles and became the Princess of Wales.

Chapter Six

ABOVE: *Prince William, less than one day old, leaves St Mary's Hospital in his mother's arms. Charles looks on admiringly.* BELOW: *The christening day.*

The Prince and Princess of Wales

FOR CLOSE ON THREE HUNDRED YEARS THE ROYAL FAMILY AND THE FAMILY of the Princess of Wales have been acquainted. Diana herself was named after an ancestor, born in 1710 who married the fourth Duke of Bedford and moved in the royal circle of that day. Lady Lyttelton, as we have seen, was brought in to rescue Queen Victoria's nursery from disaster and remained in the royal household for many years. In more recent times Cynthia, Countess Spencer, the Princess of Wales' grandmother on her father's side was a lady-in-waiting to the Queen Mother. Ruth, Lady Fermoy, her maternal grandmother, is still a lady-in-waiting to the Queen Mother. Maurice, the fourth Lord Fermoy, and King George VI, the grandfathers of Princess Diana and Prince Charles, were friends having similar interests in shooting and tennis.

In 1935 King George V leased Park House on the Sandringham estate to Lord and Lady Fermoy where, a year later, their daughter Frances was born. In 1954 Frances married Viscount Althorp, son of the seventh Earl Spencer, who was both an Equerry to King George VI and to Queen Elizabeth.

When Lord Fermoy died the family were allowed to keep on the lease of Park House and it was here in the summer of 1961 that Diana, the third daughter of Lord and Lady Althorp, was born. She was born in the room in which her mother had been born twenty-five years earlier. The previous year, Lady Althorp had given birth to a son, John, who lived only briefly. He is buried in Sandringham churchyard along with two royal children of the same name, the sons of Queen Alexandra and Queen Mary.

When Diana was six her parents separated and were later divorced; her mother going to live in London and her father remaining with his three daughters and his son, Charles, at Park House. Diana attended a small private school in King's Lynn until 1969 when it was decided that she should go to boarding school in Diss, Norfolk. Eventually she went to West Heath, a public school in Sevenoaks, where she was described as 'non-academic but cheerful, kind and outgoing'.

In 1975, on the death of her grandfather, her father became the eighth Earl Spencer inheriting Althorp Hall in Northamptonshire and its estates, and the fourteen-year-old girl became Lady Diana Spencer. When she was sixteen a request to the headmistress for a special week-end away from school was granted and Diana went to Althorp Hall. It was here that she first met Prince Charles. He and her elder sister, Sarah, who was his friend, were tramping back to the Hall after a morning's shooting. The young Diana was introduced as they walked across a muddy field. There was a difference of thirteen years between their ages, and Diana had until then only been acquainted with Prince Andrew and Prince Edward, her close contemporaries.

In 1979, after a year at a finishing school in fashionable Gstaad, Switzerland, she returned to London and was, in August, invited by Prince Andrew to Balmoral, where the royal family were spending their traditional summer holiday. There she became re-acquainted with Charles. The heir to the throne was greatly taken by the tall, fair-haired girl with lively blue eyes and a full smile. The rest of the story has been told a thousand times. Their marriage in St. Paul's Cathedral on 29 July, 1981 was one of the brilliant showpieces of the twentieth century. Millions watched it throughout the world.

In November of the same year it was announced from Buckingham Palace that the Princess of Wales was expecting a baby. Earl Spencer, the proud future grandfather enthused: 'I can't say how happy we are, Diana wanted this child. She loves young people, they adore her. She will be a marvellous mother.'

It was announced that the baby would not be born at Buckingham Palace, as so many royal children had been in the past, but in St Mary's Hospital, Paddington. This famous hospital had served the populace of one of the less fashionable boroughs of London for many years, and its excellence was well known. (It was here that the young Alexander Fleming first discovered penicillin.) Its maternity section, in the Lindo Wing, has recently acquired a high reputation. Princess Michael of Kent, amongst other royal mothers, had been one of its notable patients. It was an unusual break from tradition – never before had a future monarch been born in a public hospital. It was on the advice of Mr George Pinker, the royal gynaecologist, that the decision was finally made, and a private room was set aside for the use of the Princess.

A nanny was engaged, Barbara Barnes, who had none of the formal training of royal nannies hitherto. But she was highly recommended on the strength of her service to Colin Tennant and his wife Lady Anne, friends of Princess Margaret. Soon the presents began to arrive, innumerable pairs of bootees knitted by little girls, shawls by old ladies,

William Arthur Philip Louis photographed in December 1982. The baby prince is second in line to the throne.

*Prince William, aged six
months, with his parents.
Diana is the youngest
Princess of Wales to be a
mother since Alexandra,
who was nineteen when she
had her first child in 1864.*

toys from woodworking groups. Rather more unusual was a gift of a book of nursery rhymes made entirely in lace, the product of 10,000 working hours by the lace makers of the seaside village of Beer in Devon.

British bookmakers, ever-ready for a novelty, quoted odds of 11 to 10 on the baby being a boy, even money on a girl and 20 to 1 against twins. These latter odds had been drastically trimmed when it was realised that twins were conspicuous in the family of Princess Diana. On the Spencer side an aunt had given birth to twins in 1958, and a year earlier one of her Fermoy aunts had achieved a similar feat. Her grandfather Maurice, Lord Fermoy, was one of twins and her grandmother Ruth, Lady Fermoy was the daughter of a twin.

In the early hours of 21 June, the princess was driven from Kensington Palace to St Mary's where she entered the Lindo Wing. When the news was released later that morning, the crowds began to collect outside the hospital. Prince Charles was at his wife's bedside, and at three minutes past nine in the evening the new prince was born.

He weighed 7lb 1½oz; he had fair hair and blue eyes. Shortly afterwards the official bulletin was pinned to the railings of Buckingham Palace and the news was released. The crowds outside the Palace and the hospital celebrated in the usual British manner – by singing. The news was broadcast all over the world and flowers and tributes came flooding in.

The waiting crowd outside St Mary's was finally rewarded by the appearance of a still-bemused Prince Charles. He had been present at the birth. The proud father described the baby as 'beautiful' and 'in marvellous form'. When a voice from the crowd asked about the possibility of another baby: 'Hell,' he replied. 'Give us a chance. You ask my wife. I don't think she'll be too pleased just yet.'

Twenty-four hours later the mother and baby returned to Kensington Palace where the nursery had been made ready with modern furniture chosen by the Princess. It was hand-painted with patriotic red, white and blue rabbits.

The baby was christened William Arthur Philip Louis on 4 August in Buckingham Palace. It was a double day of celebration for it was also the 82nd birthday of his great-grandmother, Queen Elizabeth, the Queen Mother.

The lily font was brought on its traditional trip from Windsor and the infant prince wore the Honiton lace gown worn by so many royal infants at their christenings. His godparents were Princess Alexandra, ex-King Constantine of Greece, a second cousin and close friend of Prince Charles, Lord Romsey, the Duchess of Westminster, Lady Susan Hussey, a lady-in-waiting to the Queen and Laurens van der Post, the writer and friend of Prince Charles.

Prince William with Nanny Barbara Barnes en route from Australia to New Zealand.

Prince William finds his feet. The 17-month old prince with his mother in the gardens of Kensington Palace.

When it was decided that the royal couple would be embarking on a State Tour of Australia and New Zealand in the spring of 1983, Princess Diana was adamant about not leaving William for such a long period. Queen Elizabeth the Queen Mother, remembering her own separation from her daughter at eight months on a similar trip in 1927, supported Diana's determination to take the baby along, too.

Another royal precedent was achieved, and arrangements were made for the nine-month-old William, Miss Barnes and assistant nanny, Olga Powell to accompany them on the journey.

Prince William became the first ever infant heir to the throne to be included in a Royal Tour. Before he could walk and talk, he had travelled further than many of his predecessors could have dreamed.

A base was set up where William and the nannies could stay while his parents toured Australia. A ranch house at Woomargama, New South Wales, was put at their disposal by an Australian millionaire. Here William played happily in the pleasant sunshine of the Antipodean autumn, whilst his mother and father were experiencing the flies and dust of the Outback. It was here that, with the assistance of water wings and the nannies, he took his first dip in a swimming pool.

The Australians with their usual robust affection named him 'Billy the Kid'. During the tour Prince Charles and Princess Diana were bombarded with questions about the young prince, but throughout their widespread travels he stayed playing happily back at the ranch.

The family then continued on their tour to New Zealand where William put on a special performance for a throng of cameramen. In the grounds of Government House, Auckland, he crawled adventurously across a rug and even managed to stand for a few shaky seconds with the help of his father, who calls him 'Wills'. Within hours the whole world was enchanted by pictures of William. The obvious delight he gave to his parents was shared by all. 'He keeps crawling away, and his great interest is waste paper baskets,' Prince Charles was heard to comment, doubtless bringing back memories to all parents of the time when a baby suddenly becomes mobile and eager to explore everything he sees.

The royal tour of Australia and New Zealand was an outstanding success. The baby was content, the parents, particularly his mother, did not have to endure the unhappiness of separation as experienced by so many royal mothers. As Queen Victoria would have said: 'A great thing for the future.'

Queen Victoria and Prince Albert enhanced the standing of royal family life and at the same time strengthened the Throne itself. The heir to that tradition, the baby in the nursery at Kensington Palace, taking his first steps and learning his first words, will one day assume the great and regal title of King William V.

Royal walkabout in New Zealand. Prince William, with the assistance of his father, takes a few shaky steps, on the lawn of Government House, Auckland, during the triumphant Royal Tour. It was his mother's desire that he should accompany them on the long journey.

Bibliography

George Arthur, *Concerning Queen Victoria and Her Son* (Robert Hale); *Queen Alexandra* (Chapman & Hall)

Georgina Battiscombe, *Queen Alexandra* (Constable)

Hector Bolitho, *The Reign of Queen Victoria* (Collins)

Helen Cathcart, *Sandringham, The Story of a Royal Home* (W H Allen)

Virginia Cowles, *Edward VII and His Circle* (Hamish Hamilton)

Marion Crawford, *The Little Princesses* (Cassell & Co)

Taylor Darbyshire, *King George VI, An Intimate and Authentic Life* (Hutchinson)

John Dean, *HRH Prince Philip, Duke of Edinburgh, A Portrait by his Valet* (Robert Hale)

Nigel Dempster, *HRH The Princess Margaret* (Quartet)

Richard Dimbleby, *Elizabeth, Our Queen* (Hodder & Stoughton)

David Duff, *Mother of the Queen* (Muller)

Philip Gibbs (ed.), *George the Faithful – the Life and Time of George V* (Hutchinson)

J. T. Gorman, *George VI, King and Emperor* (W & G Foyle)

Robert Lacey, *Majesty* (Hutchinson)

Elizabeth Longford, *Victoria R.I.* (Weidenfeld & Nicholson)

John Matson, *Dear Osborne* (Hamish Hamilton)

Dermot Morrah, *Princess Elizabeth* (Odhams Press)

Harold Nicholson, *King George V, His Life and Reign* (Constable)

Lady Peacock, *The Queen and Her Children* (Hutchinson)

Sir Frederick Ponsonby, *Recollections of Three Reigns* (Eyre & Spottiswoode)

James Pope-Hennessy, *Queen Mary* (Allen & Unwin)

Kenneth Rose, *King George V* (Weidenfeld & Nicholson)

J. P. C. Sewell (ed.), *Personal Letters of King Edward VII* (Hutchinson)

Dorothy Margaret Stuart, *King George VI* (Harrap & Co)

Geoffrey Wakeford, *The Heir Apparent* (Robert Hale)

Sir John Wheeler-Bennett, *King George VI, His Life and Reign* (Macmillan)

The Duke of Windsor, *A King's Story* (Cassell & Co)

Cecil Woodham-Smith, *Queen Victoria, Her Life and Times, Vol. 1* (Hamish Hamilton)

Hon. Mrs Hugh Wyndham (ed.), *Correspondence of Sarah Spencer, Lady Lyttelton*

215